Amazon EC2 Auto Scaling User Guide

A catalogue record for this book is available from the Hong Kong Public Libraries.

Published in Hong Kong by Samurai Media Limited.

Email: info@samuraimedia.org

ISBN 9789888407729

Contents

What Is Amazon EC2 Auto Scaling?   **9**
    Auto Scaling Components   9
    Getting Started   10
    Accessing Auto Scaling   10
    Pricing for Auto Scaling   11
    PCI DSS Compliance   11
    Related Services   11

Benefits of Auto Scaling   **12**
    Example: Covering Variable Demand   12
    Example: Web App Architecture   14
    Example: Distributing Instances Across Availability Zones   15
        Instance Distribution   15
        Rebalancing Activities   16

Auto Scaling Lifecycle   **17**
    Scale Out   17
    Instances In Service   18
    Scale In   18
    Attach an Instance   18
    Detach an Instance   18
    Lifecycle Hooks   18
    Enter and Exit Standby   19

Auto Scaling Limits   **20**

Setting Up Amazon EC2 Auto Scaling   **21**
    Sign Up for AWS   21
    Prepare to Use Amazon EC2   21

Getting Started with Amazon EC2 Auto Scaling   **22**
    Step 1: Create a Launch Configuration   22
    Step 2: Create an Auto Scaling Group   24
    Step 3: Verify Your Auto Scaling Group   24
    Step 4: (Optional) Delete Your Scaling Infrastructure   25

Tutorial: Set Up a Scaled and Load-Balanced Application   **26**
    Prerequisites   26
    Configure Scaling and Load Balancing Using the AWS Management Console   26
        Create or Select a Launch Configuration   26
        Create an Auto Scaling Group   27
        (Optional) Verify that Your Load Balancer is Attached to Your Auto Scaling Group   28
    Configure Scaling and Load Balancing Using the AWS CLI   28
        Create a Launch Configuration   29
        Create an Auto Scaling Group with a Load Balancer   29

Launch Configurations   **30**

Creating a Launch Configuration   **31**

Creating a Launch Configuration Using an EC2 Instance   **33**
    Create a Launch Configuration Using an EC2 Instance   33
        Create a Launch Configuration from an EC2 Instance Using the AWS Management Console . . .   33

Create a Launch Configuration from an EC2 Instance Using the AWS CLI   33
Create a Launch Configuration from an Instance and Override the Block Devices   34
Create a Launch Configuration and Override the Block Devices Using the AWS CLI   34
Create a Launch Configuration and Override the Instance Type   35
Create a Launch Configuration and Override the Instance Type Using the AWS CLI   35

Changing the Launch Configuration for an Auto Scaling Group   **37**

Copying a Launch Configuration to a Launch Template   **38**

Replacing a Launch Configuration with a Launch Template   **39**

Launching Auto Scaling Instances in a VPC   **40**
Default VPC   40
IP Addressing in a VPC   40
Instance Placement Tenancy   41
Linking EC2-Classic Instances to a VPC   42
Link to a VPC Using the AWS Management Console   42
Link to a VPC Using the AWS CLI   43
Examples   43

Auto Scaling Groups   **44**

Creating an Auto Scaling Group Using a Launch Template   **45**

Creating an Auto Scaling Group Using a Launch Configuration   **47**

Creating an Auto Scaling Group Using an EC2 Instance   **49**
Create an Auto Scaling Group from an EC2 Instance Using the Console   49
Create an Auto Scaling Group from an EC2 Instance Using the AWS CLI   49

Creating an Auto Scaling Group Using the Amazon EC2 Launch Wizard   **51**

Tagging Auto Scaling Groups and Instances   **52**
Tag Restrictions   52
Tagging Lifecycle   52
Add or Modify Tags for Your Auto Scaling Group   53
Add or Modify Tags Using the AWS Management Console   53
Add or Modify Tags Using the AWS CLI   53
Delete Tags   54
Delete Tags Using the AWS Management Console   54
Delete Tags Using the AWS CLI   55

Using a Load Balancer With an Auto Scaling Group   **56**

Attaching a Load Balancer to Your Auto Scaling Group   **57**
Prerequisites   57
Add a Load Balancer Using the Console   57
Add a Load Balancer Using the AWS CLI   58

Using ELB Health Checks with Auto Scaling   **60**
Adding Health Checks Using the Console   60
Adding Health Checks Using the AWS CLI   60

Expanding Your Scaled and Load-Balanced Application to an Additional Availability Zone   **61**
Add an Availability Zone Using the Console   61
Add an Availability Zone Using the AWS CLI   62

Launching Spot Instances in Your Auto Scaling Group   **63**

Merging Your Auto Scaling Groups into a Single Multi-Zone Group   **64**
    Merge Zones Using the AWS CLI 64

Deleting Your Auto Scaling Infrastructure   **66**
    Delete Your Auto Scaling Group 66
    (Optional) Delete the Launch Configuration 66
    (Optional) Delete the Load Balancer 66
    (Optional) Delete CloudWatch Alarms 67

Scaling the Size of Your Auto Scaling Group   **68**
    Scaling Options 68
    Multiple Scaling Policies 69

Maintaining the Number of Instances in Your Auto Scaling Group   **70**
    Determining Instance Health 70
    Replacing Unhealthy Instances 70

Manual Scaling   **71**
    Change the Size of Your Auto Scaling Group Using the Console 71
    Change the Size of Your Auto Scaling Group Using the AWS CLI 71

Attach EC2 Instances to Your Auto Scaling Group   **73**
    Attaching an Instance Using the AWS Management Console 73
    Attaching an Instance Using the AWS CLI 74

Detach EC2 Instances from Your Auto Scaling Group   **77**
    Detaching Instances Using the AWS Management Console 77
    Detaching Instances Using the AWS CLI 77

Scheduled Scaling for Amazon EC2 Auto Scaling   **80**
    Considerations for Scheduled Actions 80
    Create a Scheduled Action Using the Console 80
    Update a Scheduled Action 81
    Create or Update a Scheduled Action Using the AWS CLI 81
    Delete a Scheduled Action 82

Dynamic Scaling for Amazon EC2 Auto Scaling   **83**
    Scaling Policy Types 83

Target Tracking Scaling Policies for Amazon EC2 Auto Scaling   **84**
    Considerations 84
    Create an Auto Scaling Group with Target Tracking Scaling Policies 85
    Instance Warmup 86
    Configure Scaling Policies Using the AWS CLI 86
        Step 1: Create an Auto Scaling Group 86
        Step 2: Create Scaling Policies 87

Simple and Step Scaling Policies for Amazon EC2 Auto Scaling   **88**
    Simple Scaling Policies 88
    Step Scaling Policies 88
    Scaling Adjustment Types 88
    Step Adjustments 89
    Instance Warmup 90
    Create an Auto Scaling Group with Step Scaling Policies 90

Configure Scaling Policies Using the AWS CLI 93
    Step 1: Create an Auto Scaling Group 93
    Step 2: Create Scaling Policies 93
    Step 3: Create CloudWatch Alarms 94

Add a Scaling Policy to an Existing Auto Scaling Group   **95**

Scaling Based on Amazon SQS   **96**
Scaling with Amazon SQS Using the AWS CLI 96
    Create the Scaling Policies 97
    Create the CloudWatch Alarms 97
    Verify Your Scaling Policies and CloudWatch Alarms 98
    Test Your Scale Out and Scale In Policies 98

Scaling Cooldowns for Amazon EC2 Auto Scaling   **99**
Example: Cooldowns 99
Default Cooldowns 100
Scaling-Specific Cooldowns 101
Cooldowns and Multiple Instances 101
Cooldowns and Lifecycle Hooks 101
Cooldowns and Spot Instances 102

Controlling Which Auto Scaling Instances Terminate During Scale In   **103**
Default Termination Policy 103
Customizing the Termination Policy 105
Instance Protection 106
    Enable Instance Protection for a Group 106
    Modify the Instance Protection Setting for a Group 107
    Modify the Instance Protection Setting for an Instance 108

Amazon EC2 Auto Scaling Lifecycle Hooks   **109**
How Lifecycle Hooks Work 109
Considerations When Using Lifecycle Hooks 110
    Keeping Instances in a Wait State 110
    Cooldowns and Custom Actions 111
    Health Check Grace Period 111
    Lifecycle Action Result 111
    Spot Instances 111
Prepare for Notifications 111
    Receive Notification Using CloudWatch Events 112
    Receive Notification Using Amazon SNS 112
    Receive Notification Using Amazon SQS 113
Add Lifecycle Hooks 113
Complete the Lifecycle Hook 114
Test the Notification 114

Temporarily Removing Instances from Your Auto Scaling Group   **116**
How the Standby State Works 116
Health Status of an Instance in a Standby State 117
Temporarily Remove an Instance Using the AWS Management Console 117
Temporarily Remove an Instance Using the AWS CLI 117

Suspending and Resuming Scaling Processes   **120**
Scaling Processes 120
Suspend and Resume Processes Using the Console 121
Suspend and Resume Processes Using the AWS CLI 121

Monitoring Your Auto Scaling Instances and Groups   **123**

Health Checks for Auto Scaling Instances   **124**
Instance Health Status 124
Health Check Grace Period 124
Custom Health Checks 124

Monitoring Your Auto Scaling Groups and Instances Using Amazon CloudWatch   **126**
Auto Scaling Group Metrics 126
Dimensions for Auto Scaling Group Metrics 127
Enable Auto Scaling Group Metrics 127
Configure Monitoring for Auto Scaling Instances 128
View CloudWatch Metrics 128
Create Amazon CloudWatch Alarms 129

Getting CloudWatch Events When Your Auto Scaling Group Scales   **131**
Auto Scaling Events 131
    EC2 Instance-launch Lifecycle Action 131
    EC2 Instance Launch Successful 132
    EC2 Instance Launch Unsuccessful 132
    EC2 Instance-terminate Lifecycle Action 133
    EC2 Instance Terminate Successful 133
    EC2 Instance Terminate Unsuccessful 134
Create a Lambda Function 135
Route Events to Your Lambda Function 135

Getting SNS Notifications When Your Auto Scaling Group Scales   **137**
SNS Notifications 137
Configure Amazon SNS 138
    Create an Amazon SNS Topic 138
    Subscribe to the Amazon SNS Topic 138
    Confirm Your Amazon SNS Subscription 138
Configure Your Auto Scaling Group to Send Notifications 138
Test the Notification Configuration 139
Verify That You Received Notification of the Scaling Event 140
Delete the Notification Configuration 141

Logging Amazon EC2 Auto Scaling API Calls By Using AWS CloudTrail   **142**
Auto Scaling Information in CloudTrail 142
Understanding Auto Scaling Log File Entries 142

Controlling Access to Your Amazon EC2 Auto Scaling Resources   **145**
Amazon EC2 Auto Scaling Actions 145
    Required Permissions 146
Amazon EC2 Auto Scaling Resources 146
Amazon EC2 Auto Scaling Condition Keys 147
Supported Resource-Level Permissions 147
Predefined AWS Managed Policies 149
Customer Managed Policies 149
    Example: Require a Launch Template 149
    Example: Create and Manage Launch Configurations 150
    Example: Create and Manage Auto Scaling Groups and Scaling Policies 151
    Example: Control Access Using Tags 152
    Example: Change the Capacity of Auto Scaling Groups 154

Service-Linked Roles for Amazon EC2 Auto Scaling   **155**

Permissions Granted by AWSServiceRoleForAutoScaling 155
Create the Service-Linked Role 155
Edit the Service-Linked Role 156
Delete the Service-Linked Role 156

Launch Auto Scaling Instances with an IAM Role   **157**
Prerequisites 157
Create a Launch Configuration 157

Troubleshooting Amazon EC2 Auto Scaling   **158**
Retrieving an Error Message 158

Troubleshooting Amazon EC2 Auto Scaling: EC2 Instance Launch Failures   **160**
The security group does not exist. Launching EC2 instance failed. 160
The key pair does not exist. Launching EC2 instance failed. 160
The requested configuration is currently not supported. 161
AutoScalingGroup not found. 161
The requested Availability Zone is no longer supported. Please retry your request 161
Your requested instance type () is not supported in your requested Availability Zone (). 161
You are not subscribed to this service. Please see http://aws/.amazon/.com/. 161
Invalid device name upload. Launching EC2 instance failed. 161
Value () for parameter virtualName is invalid... 162
EBS block device mappings not supported for instance-store AMIs. 162
Placement groups may not be used with instances of type 'm1.large'. Launching EC2 instance failed. . 162

Troubleshooting Amazon EC2 Auto Scaling: AMI Issues   **163**
The AMI ID does not exist. Launching EC2 instance failed. 163
AMI is pending, and cannot be run. Launching EC2 instance failed. 163
Value () for parameter virtualName is invalid. 163
The requested instance type's architecture (i386) does not match the architecture in the manifest for
    ami-6622f00f (x86_64). Launching ec2 instance failed. 163

Troubleshooting Amazon EC2 Auto Scaling: Load Balancer Issues   **165**
Cannot find Load Balancer . Validating load balancer configuration failed. 165
There is no ACTIVE Load Balancer named . Updating load balancer configuration failed. 165
EC2 instance is not in VPC. Updating load balancer configuration failed. 165
EC2 instance is in VPC. Updating load balancer configuration failed. 165
The security token included in the request is invalid. Validating load balancer configuration failed. . . 166

Troubleshooting Auto Scaling: Capacity Limits   **167**
We currently do not have sufficient capacity in the Availability Zone you requested (). 167
 instance(s) are already running. Launching EC2 instance failed. 167

Auto Scaling Resources   **168**

Document History   **169**

What Is Amazon EC2 Auto Scaling?

Amazon EC2 Auto Scaling helps you ensure that you have the correct number of Amazon EC2 instances available to handle the load for your application. You create collections of EC2 instances, called *Auto Scaling groups*. You can specify the minimum number of instances in each Auto Scaling group, and Auto Scaling ensures that your group never goes below this size. You can specify the maximum number of instances in each Auto Scaling group, and Auto Scaling ensures that your group never goes above this size. If you specify the desired capacity, either when you create the group or at any time thereafter, Auto Scaling ensures that your group has this many instances. If you specify scaling policies, then Auto Scaling can launch or terminate instances as demand on your application increases or decreases.

For example, the following Auto Scaling group has a minimum size of 1 instance, a desired capacity of 2 instances, and a maximum size of 4 instances. The scaling policies that you define adjust the number of instances, within your minimum and maximum number of instances, based on the criteria that you specify.

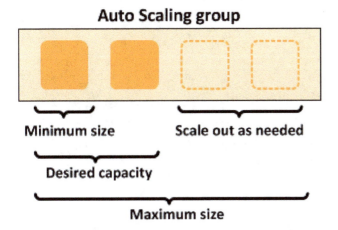

For more information about the benefits of Auto Scaling, see Benefits of Auto Scaling.

Auto Scaling Components

The following table describes the key components of Auto Scaling.

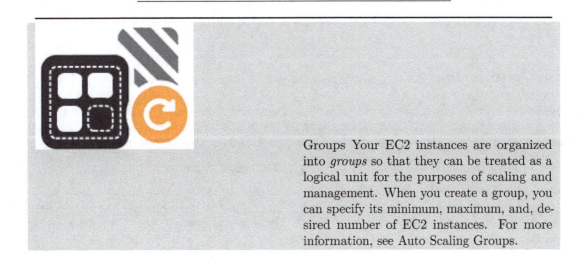

Groups Your EC2 instances are organized into *groups* so that they can be treated as a logical unit for the purposes of scaling and management. When you create a group, you can specify its minimum, maximum, and, desired number of EC2 instances. For more information, see Auto Scaling Groups.

Launch configurations Your group uses a *launch configuration* as a template for its EC2 instances. When you create a launch configuration, you can specify information such as the AMI ID, instance type, key pair, security groups, and block device mapping for your instances. For more information, see Launch Configurations.

Scaling plans A *scaling plan* tells Auto Scaling when and how to scale. For example, you can base a scaling plan on the occurrence of specified conditions (dynamic scaling) or on a schedule. For more information, see Scaling Options.

Getting Started

If you're new to Auto Scaling, we recommend that you review Auto Scaling Lifecycle before you begin.

To begin, complete the Getting Started with Amazon EC2 Auto Scaling tutorial to create an Auto Scaling group and see how it responds when an instance in that group terminates. If you already have running EC2 instances, you can create an Auto Scaling group using an existing EC2 instance, and remove the instance from the group at any time.

Accessing Auto Scaling

AWS provides a web-based user interface, the AWS Management Console. If you've signed up for an AWS account, you can access Auto Scaling by signing into the AWS Management Console. To get started, choose **EC2** from the console home page, and then choose **Launch Configurations** from the navigation pane.

If you prefer to use a command line interface, you have the following options:

AWS Command Line Interface (CLI)
Provides commands for a broad set of AWS products, and is supported on Windows, Mac, and Linux. To get started, see AWS Command Line Interface User Guide. For more information about the commands for Auto Scaling, see autoscaling in the *AWS CLI Command Reference*.

AWS Tools for Windows PowerShell
Provides commands for a broad set of AWS products for those who script in the PowerShell environment. To get

started, see the AWS Tools for Windows PowerShell User Guide. For more information about the cmdlets for Auto Scaling, see the AWS Tools for PowerShell Cmdlet Reference.

Auto Scaling provides a Query API. These requests are HTTP or HTTPS requests that use the HTTP verbs GET or POST and a Query parameter named `Action`. For more information about the API actions for Auto Scaling, see Actions in the *Amazon EC2 Auto Scaling API Reference.*

If you prefer to build applications using language-specific APIs instead of submitting a request over HTTP or HTTPS, AWS provides libraries, sample code, tutorials, and other resources for software developers. These libraries provide basic functions that automate tasks such as cryptographically signing your requests, retrying requests, and handling error responses, making it is easier for you to get started. For more information, see AWS SDKs and Tools.

For information about your credentials for accessing AWS, see AWS Security Credentials in the *Amazon Web Services General Reference.*

Pricing for Auto Scaling

There are no additional fees with Auto Scaling, so it's easy to try it out and see how it can benefit your AWS architecture.

PCI DSS Compliance

Auto Scaling supports the processing, storage, and transmission of credit card data by a merchant or service provider, and has been validated as being compliant with Payment Card Industry (PCI) Data Security Standard (DSS). For more information about PCI DSS, including how to request a copy of the AWS PCI Compliance Package, see PCI DSS Level 1.

Related Services

To configure automatic scaling for all of the scalable resources for your application, use AWS Auto Scaling. For more information, see the AWS Auto Scaling User Guide.

To automatically distribute incoming application traffic across multiple instances in your Auto Scaling group, use Elastic Load Balancing. For more information, see the Elastic Load Balancing User Guide.

To monitor basic statistics for your instances and Amazon EBS volumes, use Amazon CloudWatch. For more information, see the Amazon CloudWatch User Guide.

To monitor the calls made to the Auto Scaling API for your account, including calls made by the AWS Management Console, command line tools, and other services, use AWS CloudTrail. For more information, see the AWS CloudTrail User Guide.

Benefits of Auto Scaling

Adding Auto Scaling to your application architecture is one way to maximize the benefits of the AWS cloud. When you use Auto Scaling, your applications gain the following benefits:

- Better fault tolerance. Auto Scaling can detect when an instance is unhealthy, terminate it, and launch an instance to replace it. You can also configure Auto Scaling to use multiple Availability Zones. If one Availability Zone becomes unavailable, Auto Scaling can launch instances in another one to compensate.
- Better availability. Auto Scaling can help you ensure that your application always has the right amount of capacity to handle the current traffic demand.
- Better cost management. Auto Scaling can dynamically increase and decrease capacity as needed. Because you pay for the EC2 instances you use, you save money by launching instances when they are actually needed and terminating them when they aren't needed.

Topics

- Example: Covering Variable Demand
- Example: Web App Architecture
- Example: Distributing Instances Across Availability Zones

Example: Covering Variable Demand

To demonstrate some of the benefits of Auto Scaling, consider a basic Web application running on AWS. This application allows employees to search for conference rooms that they might want to use for meetings. During the beginning and end of the week, usage of this application is minimal. During the middle of the week, more employees are scheduling meetings, so the demand on the application increases significantly.

The following graph shows how much of the application's capacity is used over the course of a week.

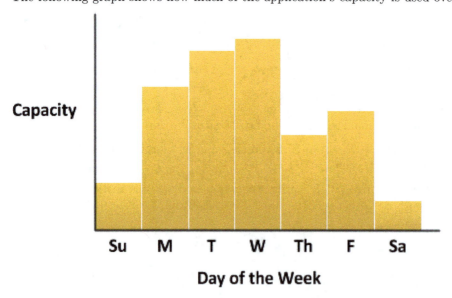

Traditionally, there are two ways to plan for these changes in capacity. The first option is to add enough servers so that the application always has enough capacity to meet demand. The downside of this option, however, is that there are days in which the application doesn't need this much capacity. The extra capacity remains unused and, in essence, raises the cost of keeping the application running.

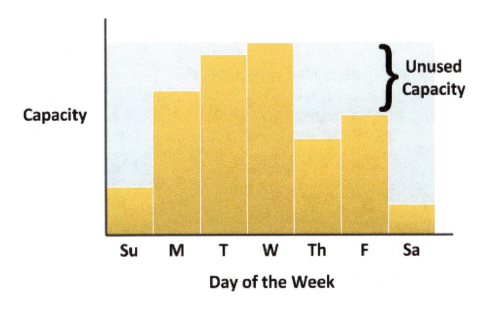

Capacity

Su M T W Th F Sa

Day of the Week

▢ Available Capacity

The second option is to have enough capacity to handle the average demand on the application. This option is less expensive, because you aren't purchasing equipment that you'll only use occasionally. However, you risk creating a poor customer experience when the demand on the application exceeds its capacity.

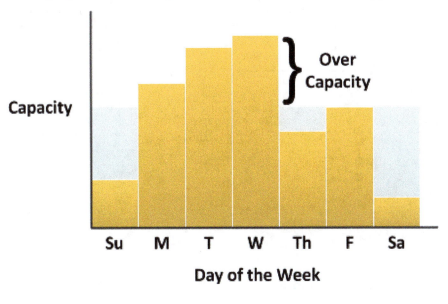

Capacity

Su M T W Th F Sa

Day of the Week

▢ Available Capacity

By adding Auto Scaling to this application, you have a third option available. You can add new instances to the application only when necessary, and terminate them when they're no longer needed. Because Auto Scaling uses EC2 instances, you only have to pay for the instances you use, when you use them. You now have a cost-effective architecture that provides the best customer experience while minimizing expenses.

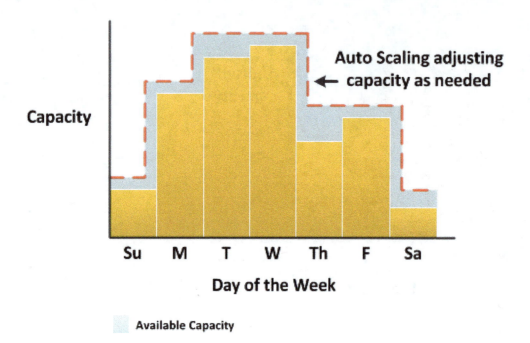

Capacity

Auto Scaling adjusting
← capacity as needed

Su   M   T   W   Th   F   Sa

Day of the Week

Available Capacity

Example: Web App Architecture

In a common web app scenario, you run multiple copies of your app simultaneously to cover the volume of your customer traffic. These multiple copies of your application are hosted on identical EC2 instances (cloud servers), each handling customer requests.

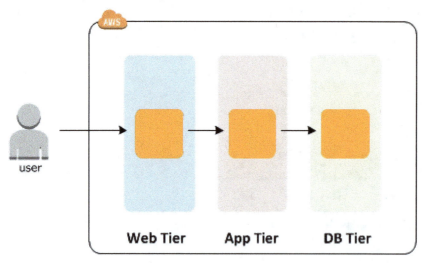

Auto Scaling manages the launch and termination of these EC2 instances on your behalf. You define a set of criteria (such as an Amazon CloudWatch alarm) that determines when the Auto Scaling group launches or terminates EC2 instances. Adding Auto Scaling groups to your network architecture can help you make your application more highly available and fault tolerant.

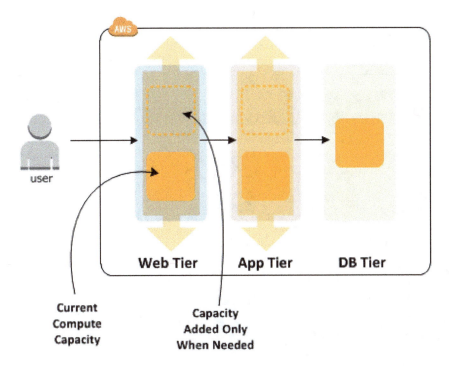

You can create as many Auto Scaling groups as you need. For example, you can create an Auto Scaling group for each tier.

You can create as many Auto Scaling groups as you need. For example, you can create an Auto Scaling group for each tier.

To distribute traffic between the instances in your Auto Scaling groups, you can introduce a load balancer into your architecture. For more information, see Using a Load Balancer With an Auto Scaling Group.

Example: Distributing Instances Across Availability Zones

AWS resources, such as EC2 instances, are housed in highly-available data centers. To provide additional scalability and reliability, these data centers are in different physical locations. *Regions* are large and widely dispersed geographic locations. Each region contains multiple distinct locations, called *Availability Zones*, that are engineered to be isolated from failures in other Availability Zones and provide inexpensive, low-latency network connectivity to other Availability Zones in the same region. For more information, see Regions and Endpoints: Auto Scaling in the *Amazon Web Services General Reference*.

Auto Scaling enables you to take advantage of the safety and reliability of geographic redundancy by spanning Auto Scaling groups across multiple Availability Zones within a region. When one Availability Zone becomes unhealthy or unavailable, Auto Scaling launches new instances in an unaffected Availability Zone. When the unhealthy Availability Zone returns to a healthy state, Auto Scaling automatically redistributes the application instances evenly across all of the designated Availability Zones.

An Auto Scaling group can contain EC2 instances in one or more Availability Zones within the same region. However, Auto Scaling groups cannot span multiple regions.

For Auto Scaling groups in a VPC, the EC2 instances are launched in subnets. You select the subnets for your EC2 instances when you create or update the Auto Scaling group. You can select one or more subnets per Availability Zone. For more information, see Launching Auto Scaling Instances in a VPC.

Instance Distribution

Auto Scaling attempts to distribute instances evenly between the Availability Zones that are enabled for your Auto Scaling group. Auto Scaling does this by attempting to launch new instances in the Availability Zone with the fewest instances. If the attempt fails, however, Auto Scaling attempts to launch the instances in another

Availability Zone until it succeeds. For Auto Scaling groups in a VPC, if there are multiple subnets in an Availability Zone, Auto Scaling selects a subnet from the Availability Zone at random.

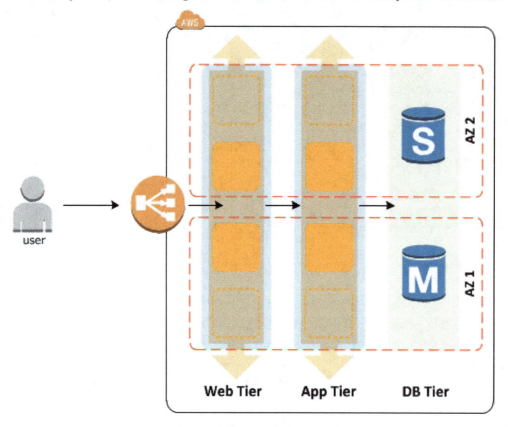

Rebalancing Activities

After certain actions occur, your Auto Scaling group can become unbalanced between Availability Zones. Auto Scaling compensates by rebalancing the Availability Zones. The following actions can lead to rebalancing activity:

- You change the Availability Zones for your group.
- You explicitly terminate or detach instances and the group becomes unbalanced.
- An Availability Zone that previously had insufficient capacity recovers and has additional capacity available.
- An Availability Zone that previously had a Spot market price above your Spot bid price now has a market price below your bid price.

When rebalancing, Auto Scaling launches new instances before terminating the old ones, so that rebalancing does not compromise the performance or availability of your application.

Because Auto Scaling attempts to launch new instances before terminating the old ones, being at or near the specified maximum capacity could impede or completely halt rebalancing activities. To avoid this problem, the system can temporarily exceed the specified maximum capacity of a group by a 10 percent margin (or by a 1-instance margin, whichever is greater) during a rebalancing activity. The margin is extended only if the group is at or near maximum capacity and needs rebalancing, either because of user-requested rezoning or to compensate for zone availability issues. The extension lasts only as long as needed to rebalance the group typically a few minutes.

Auto Scaling Lifecycle

The EC2 instances in an Auto Scaling group have a path, or lifecycle, that differs from that of other EC2 instances. The lifecycle starts when the Auto Scaling group launches an instance and puts it into service. The lifecycle ends when you terminate the instance, or the Auto Scaling group takes the instance out of service and terminates it.

Note
You are billed for instances as soon as they are launched, including the time that they are not yet in service.

The following illustration shows the transitions between instance states in the Auto Scaling lifecycle.

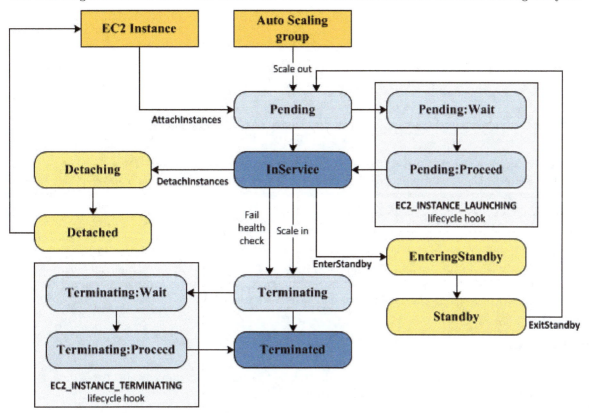

Scale Out

The following scale out events direct the Auto Scaling group to launch EC2 instances and attach them to the group:

- You manually increase the size of the group. For more information, see Manual Scaling.
- You create a scaling policy to automatically increase the size of the group based on a specified increase in demand. For more information, see Dynamic Scaling for Amazon EC2 Auto Scaling.
- You set up scaling by schedule to increase the size of the group at a specific time. For more information, see Scheduled Scaling for Amazon EC2 Auto Scaling.

When a scale out event occurs, the Auto Scaling group launches the required number of EC2 instances, using its assigned launch configuration. These instances start in the `Pending` state. If you add a lifecycle hook to your Auto Scaling group, you can perform a custom action here. For more information, see Lifecycle Hooks.

When each instance is fully configured and passes the Amazon EC2 health checks, it is attached to the Auto Scaling group and it enters the `InService` state. The instance is counted against the desired capacity of the Auto Scaling group.

Instances In Service

Instances remain in the `InService` state until one of the following occurs:

- A scale in event occurs, and Auto Scaling chooses to terminate this instance in order to reduce the size of the Auto Scaling group. For more information, see Controlling Which Auto Scaling Instances Terminate During Scale In.
- You put the instance into a `Standby` state. For more information, see Enter and Exit Standby.
- You detach the instance from the Auto Scaling group. For more information, see Detach an Instance.
- The instance fails a required number of health checks, so it is removed from the Auto Scaling group, terminated, and replaced. For more information, see Health Checks for Auto Scaling Instances.

Scale In

It is important that you create a corresponding scale in event for each scale out event that you create. This helps ensure that the resources assigned to your application match the demand for those resources as closely as possible.

The following scale in events direct the Auto Scaling group to detach EC2 instances from the group and terminate them:

- You manually decrease the size of the group.
- You create a scaling policy to automatically decrease the size of the group based on a specified decrease in demand.
- You set up scaling by schedule to decrease the size of the group at a specific time.

When a scale in event occurs, the Auto Scaling group detaches one or more instances. The Auto Scaling group uses its termination policy to determine which instances to terminate. Instances that are in the process of detaching from the Auto Scaling group and shutting down enter the `Terminating` state, and can't be put back into service. If you add a lifecycle hook to your Auto Scaling group, you can perform a custom action here. Finally, the instances are completely terminated and enter the `Terminated` state.

Attach an Instance

You can attach a running EC2 instance that meets certain criteria to your Auto Scaling group. After the instance is attached, it is managed as part of the Auto Scaling group.

For more information, see Attach EC2 Instances to Your Auto Scaling Group.

Detach an Instance

You can detach an instance from your Auto Scaling group. After the instance is detached, you can manage it separately from the Auto Scaling group or attach it to a different Auto Scaling group.

For more information, see Detach EC2 Instances from Your Auto Scaling Group.

Lifecycle Hooks

You can add a lifecycle hook to your Auto Scaling group so that you can perform custom actions when instances launch or terminate.

When Auto Scaling responds to a scale out event, it launches one or more instances. These instances start in the `Pending` state. If you added an `autoscaling:EC2_INSTANCE_LAUNCHING` lifecycle hook to your Auto Scaling group, the instances move from the `Pending` state to the `Pending:Wait` state. After you complete the lifecycle action, the instances enter the `Pending:Proceed` state. When the instances are fully configured, they are attached to the Auto Scaling group and they enter the `InService` state.

When Auto Scaling responds to a scale in event, it terminates one or more instances. These instances are detached from the Auto Scaling group and enter the `Terminating` state. If you added an `autoscaling:EC2_INSTANCE_TERMINATING` lifecycle hook to your Auto Scaling group, the instances move from the `Terminating` state to the `Terminating:Wait` state. After you complete the lifecycle action, the instances enter the `Terminating:Proceed` state. When the instances are fully terminated, they enter the `Terminated` state.

For more information, see Amazon EC2 Auto Scaling Lifecycle Hooks.

Enter and Exit Standby

You can put any instance that is in an `InService` state into a `Standby` state. This enables you to remove the instance from service, troubleshoot or make changes to it, and then put it back into service.

Instances in a `Standby` state continue to be managed by the Auto Scaling group. However, they are not an active part of your application until you put them back into service.

For more information, see Temporarily Removing Instances from Your Auto Scaling Group.

Auto Scaling Limits

To view the current limits for your Auto Scaling resources, use the **Limits** page of the Amazon EC2 console or the describe-account-limits (AWS CLI) command. To request a limit increase, use the Auto Scaling Limits form.

The following limits are related to your Auto Scaling resources.

Regional Limits

- Launch configurations per region: 200
- Auto Scaling groups per region: 200

Auto Scaling Group Limits

- Scaling policies per Auto Scaling group: 50
- Scheduled actions per Auto Scaling group: 125
- Lifecycle hooks per Auto Scaling group: 50
- SNS topics per Auto Scaling group: 10
- Classic Load Balancers per Auto Scaling group: 50
- Target groups per Auto Scaling group: 50

Scaling Policy Limits

- Step adjustments per scaling policy: 20

Auto Scaling API Limits

- You can use AttachInstances, DetachInstances, EnterStandby, and ExitStandby with at most 20 instance IDs at a time.
- You can use AttachLoadBalancers and DetachLoadBalancers with at most 10 load balancers at a time.
- You can use AttachLoadBalancerTargetGroups and DetachLoadBalancerTargetGroups with at most 10 target groups at a time.

Setting Up Amazon EC2 Auto Scaling

Before you start using Amazon EC2 Auto Scaling, complete the following tasks.

Topics

- Sign Up for AWS
- Prepare to Use Amazon EC2

Sign Up for AWS

When you create an AWS account, we automatically sign up your account for all AWS services. You pay only for the services that you use. You can use Amazon EC2 Auto Scaling at no additional charge beyond what you are paying for your EC2 instances.

If you don't have an AWS account, sign up for AWS as follows.

To sign up for an AWS account

1. Open https://aws.amazon.com/, and then choose **Create an AWS Account**. **Note**
   This might be unavailable in your browser if you previously signed into the AWS Management Console. In that case, choose **Sign in to a different account**, and then choose **Create a new AWS account**.

2. Follow the online instructions.

   Part of the sign-up procedure involves receiving a phone call and entering a PIN using the phone keypad.

AWS sends you a confirmation e-mail after the sign-up process is complete.

Prepare to Use Amazon EC2

If you haven't used Amazon EC2 before, complete the tasks described in the Amazon EC2 documentation. For more information, see Setting Up with Amazon EC2 in the *Amazon EC2 User Guide for Linux Instances* or Setting Up with Amazon EC2 in the *Amazon EC2 User Guide for Windows Instances*, depending on which operating system you plan to use for your EC2 instances.

Getting Started with Amazon EC2 Auto Scaling

When you use Amazon EC2 Auto Scaling, you must use certain building blocks to get started. This tutorial walks you through the process for setting up the basic infrastructure for Amazon EC2 Auto Scaling.

The following step-by-step instructions help you create a configuration that defines your EC2 instances, create an Auto Scaling group to maintain the healthy number of instances at all times, and optionally delete this basic infrastructure. This tutorial assumes that you are familiar with launching EC2 instances and have already created a key pair and a security group.

If you created a launch template, you can use your launch template to create an Auto Scaling group instead of creating a launch configuration. For more information, see Creating an Auto Scaling Group Using a Launch Template.

Topics

- Step 1: Create a Launch Configuration
- Step 2: Create an Auto Scaling Group
- Step 3: Verify Your Auto Scaling Group
- Step 4: (Optional) Delete Your Scaling Infrastructure

Step 1: Create a Launch Configuration

A launch configuration specifies the type of EC2 instance that Amazon EC2 Auto Scaling creates for you. You create the launch configuration by including information such as the ID of the Amazon Machine Image (AMI) to use, the instance type, the key pair, security groups, and block device mapping.

To create a launch configuration

1. Open the Amazon EC2 console at https://console.aws.amazon.com/ec2/.

2. On the navigation bar, select a region. The Auto Scaling resources that you create are tied to the region you specify and are not replicated across regions. For more information, see Example: Distributing Instances Across Availability Zones.

3. On the navigation pane, under **Auto Scaling**, choose **Auto Scaling Groups**.

4. On the **Welcome to Auto Scaling** page, choose **Create Auto Scaling group**.

Welcome to Auto Scaling

You can use Auto Scaling to manage Amazon EC2 capacity automatically, maintain the right number of instances for your application, operate a healthy group of instances, and scale it according to your needs.
Learn more

Create Auto Scaling group

Note: To create your Auto Scaling groups in a different region, select your region from the navigation bar.

Benefits of Auto Scaling

Reusable Instance Templates

Provision instances based on a reusable template you define, called a launch configuration.

Learn more

Automated Provisioning

Keep your Auto Scaling group healthy and balanced, whether you need one instance or 1,000.

Learn more

Adjustable Capacity

Maintain a fixed group size or adjust dynamically based on Amazon CloudWatch metrics.

Learn more

5. On the **Create Auto Scaling Group** page, choose **Launch Configuration, Create a new launch configuration**, and then choose **Next Step**.

6. For the **Choose AMI** step, there is a list of basic configurations, called Amazon Machine Images (AMIs), that serve as templates for your instance. Choose **Select** for the Amazon Linux AMI.

7. For the **Choose Instance Type** step, select a hardware configuration for your instance. We recommend that you keep the default, a t2.micro instance. Choose **Next: Configure details. Note** T2 instances must be launched into a subnet of a VPC. If you select a t2.micro instance but don't have a VPC, one is created for you. This VPC includes a public subnet in each Availability Zone in the region.

8. For the **Configure details** step, do the following:

   1. For **Name**, type a name for your launch configuration (for example, my-first-lc).

   2. For **Advanced Details**, select an IP address type. If you want to connect to an instance in a VPC, you must select an option that assigns a public IP address. If you want to connect to your instance but aren't sure whether you have a default VPC, select **Assign a public IP address to every instance**.

   3. Choose **Skip to review**.

9. For the **Review** step, choose **Edit security groups**. Follow the instructions to choose an existing security group, and then choose **Review**.

10. For the **Review** step, choose **Create launch configuration**.

11. Complete the **Select an existing key pair or create a new key pair** step as instructed. Note that you won't connect to your instance as part of this tutorial. Therefore, you can select **Proceed without a key pair** unless you intend to connect to your instance.

12. Choose **Create launch configuration**. The launch configuration is created and the wizard to create an Auto Scaling group is displayed.

Step 2: Create an Auto Scaling Group

An Auto Scaling group is a collection of EC2 instances, and the core of Amazon EC2 Auto Scaling. When you create an Auto Scaling group, you include information such as the subnets for the instances and the number of instances the group must maintain at all times.

Use the following procedure to continue where you left off after creating the launch configuration.

To create an Auto Scaling group

1. For the **Configure Auto Scaling group details** step, do the following:

   1. For **Group name**, type a name for your Auto Scaling group (for example, `my-first-asg`).

   2. Keep **Group size** set to the default value of 1 instance for this tutorial.

   3. Keep **Network** set to the default VPC for the region, or select your own VPC.

   4. For **Subnet**, select one or more subnets for your Auto Scaling instances.

   5. Choose **Next: Configure scaling policies**.

2. On the **Configure scaling policies** page, select **Keep this group at its initial size** and choose **Review**.

3. On the **Review** page, choose **Create Auto Scaling group**.

4. On the **Auto Scaling group creation status** page, choose **Close**.

Step 3: Verify Your Auto Scaling Group

Now that you have created your Auto Scaling group, you are ready to verify that the group has launched an EC2 instance.

To verify that your Auto Scaling group has launched an EC2 instance

1. On the **Auto Scaling Groups** page, select the Auto Scaling group that you just created.

2. On the **Activity History** tab, the **Status** column shows the current status of your instance. While your instance is launching, the status column shows `In progress`. The status changes to `Successful` after the instance is launched. You can also use the refresh button to see the current status of your instance.

3. On the **Instances** tab, the **Lifecycle** column shows the state of your instance. You can see that your Auto Scaling group has launched your EC2 instance, and that it is in the `InService` lifecycle state. The **Health Status** column shows the result of the EC2 instance health check on your instance.

4. (Optional) If you want, you can try the following experiment to learn more about Amazon EC2 Auto Scaling. The minimum size for your Auto Scaling group is 1 instance. Therefore, if you terminate the running instance, Amazon EC2 Auto Scaling must launch a new instance to replace it.

   1. On the **Instances** tab, select the ID of the instance. This shows you the instance on the **Instances** page.

   2. Choose **Actions, Instance State, Terminate**. When prompted for confirmation, choose **Yes, Terminate**.

   3. On the navigation pane, choose **Auto Scaling Groups**. Select your Auto Scaling group and choose the **Activity History** tab. The default cooldown for the Auto Scaling group is 300 seconds (5 minutes), so it takes about 5 minutes until you see the scaling activity. When the scaling activity starts, you'll see an entry for the termination of the first instance and an entry for the launch of a new instance. The **Instances** tab shows the new instance only.

   4. On the navigation pane, choose **Instances**. This page shows both the terminated instance and the running instance.

Go to the next step if you would like to delete your basic infrastructure for automatic scaling. Otherwise, you can use this infrastructure as your base and try one or more of the following:

- Maintaining the Number of Instances in Your Auto Scaling Group
- Manual Scaling
- Dynamic Scaling for Amazon EC2 Auto Scaling
- Getting SNS Notifications When Your Auto Scaling Group Scales

Step 4: (Optional) Delete Your Scaling Infrastructure

You can either delete your scaling infrastructure or delete just your Auto Scaling group and keep your launch template to use at a later time.

To delete your Auto Scaling group

1. Open the Amazon EC2 console at https://console.aws.amazon.com/ec2/.

2. On the navigation pane, under **Auto Scaling**, choose **Auto Scaling Groups**.

3. Select your Auto Scaling group (for example, **my-first-asg**).

4. Choose **Actions**, **Delete**. When prompted for confirmation, choose **Yes, Delete**.

   The **Name** column indicates that the Auto Scaling group is being deleted. The **Desired**, **Min**, and **Max** columns shows 0 instances for the Auto Scaling group.

Skip this procedure if you would like keep your launch configuration.

To delete your launch configuration

1. On the navigation pane, under **Auto Scaling**, choose **Launch Configurations**.

2. Select your launch configuration (for example, my-first-lc).

3. Choose **Actions**, **Delete launch configuration**. When prompted for confirmation, choose **Yes, Delete**.

Tutorial: Set Up a Scaled and Load-Balanced Application

You can attach a load balancer to your Auto Scaling group. The load balancer automatically distributes incoming traffic across the instances in the group. For more information about the benefits of using Elastic Load Balancing with Auto Scaling, see Using a Load Balancer With an Auto Scaling Group.

This tutorial attaches a load balancer to an Auto Scaling group when you create the group. To attach a load balancer to an existing Auto Scaling group, see Attaching a Load Balancer to Your Auto Scaling Group.

Topics

- Prerequisites
- Configure Scaling and Load Balancing Using the AWS Management Console
- Configure Scaling and Load Balancing Using the AWS CLI

Prerequisites

- (Optional) Create an IAM role that grants your application the access to AWS that it needs.

- Launch an instance; be sure to specify the IAM role (if you created one) and specify any configuration scripts that you need as user data. Connect to the instance and customize it. For example, you can install software and applications and copy data. Test your application on your instance to ensure that your instance is configured correctly. Create a custom Amazon Machine Image (AMI) from your instance. You can terminate the instance if you no longer need it.

- Create a load balancer. Elastic Load Balancing supports three types of load balancers: Application Load Balancers, Network Load Balancers, and Classic Load Balancers. You can attach any of these types of load balancers to your Auto Scaling group. For more information, see the Elastic Load Balancing User Guide.

  With Classic Load Balancers, instances are registered with the load balancer. With Application Load Balancers and Network Load Balancers, instances are registered as targets with a target group. When you plan to use your load balancer with an Auto Scaling group, you don't need to register your EC2 instances with the load balancer or target group. After you attach a load balancer or target group to your Auto Scaling group, Auto Scaling registers your instances with the load balancer or target group when it launches them.

Configure Scaling and Load Balancing Using the AWS Management Console

Complete the following tasks to set up a scaled and load-balanced application when you create your Auto Scaling group.

Topics

- Create or Select a Launch Configuration
- Create an Auto Scaling Group
- (Optional) Verify that Your Load Balancer is Attached to Your Auto Scaling Group

Create or Select a Launch Configuration

A launch configuration specifies the type of EC2 instance that Amazon EC2 Auto Scaling creates for you. When you create a launch configuration, you include information such as the ID of the Amazon Machine Image (AMI) to use, the instance type, key pair, and block device mapping. If you created a launch template, you can use your launch template to create an Auto Scaling group instead of using a launch configuration. For more information, see Creating an Auto Scaling Group Using a Launch Template.

If you already have a launch configuration that you'd like to use, select it using the following procedure.

To select an existing launch configuration

1. Open the Amazon EC2 console at https://console.aws.amazon.com/ec2/.

2. On the navigation bar at the top of the screen, select the region that you used when creating your load balancer.

3. On the navigation pane, under **Auto Scaling**, choose **Auto Scaling Groups**.

4. On the next page, choose **Create Auto Scaling group**.

5. On the **Create Auto Scaling Group** page, choose **Launch Configuration**, select an existing launch configuration, and then choose **Next Step**.

To create a new launch configuration, use the following procedure:

To create a launch configuration

1. Open the Amazon EC2 console at https://console.aws.amazon.com/ec2/.

2. On the navigation bar at the top of the screen, select the region that you used when creating your load balancer.

3. On the navigation pane, under **Auto Scaling**, choose **Auto Scaling Groups**.

4. On the next page, choose **Create Auto Scaling group**.

5. On the **Create Auto Scaling Group** page, choose **Launch Configuration, Create a new launch configuration**, and then choose **Next Step**.

6. On the **Choose AMI** page, select your custom AMI.

7. On the **Choose Instance Type** page, select a hardware configuration for your instance, and then choose **Next: Configure details**.

8. On the **Configure Details** page, do the following:

   1. For **Name**, type a name for your launch configuration.

   2. (Optional) To securely distribute credentials to your EC2 instance, select your IAM role.

   3. (Optional) If you need to connect to an instance in a nondefault VPC, for **Advanced Details, IP Address Type**, choose **Assign a public IP address to every instance**.

   4. (Optional) To specify user data or a configuration script for your instance, for **Advanced Details, User data**, paste your configuration script.

   5. Choose **Skip to review**.

9. On the **Review** page, choose **Edit security groups**. Follow the instructions to choose an existing security group, and then choose **Review**.

10. On the **Review** page, choose **Create launch configuration**.

11. On the **Select an existing key pair or create a new key pair** page, select one of the listed options. Select the acknowledgment check box, and then choose **Create launch configuration. Warning** Do not choose **Proceed without a key pair** if you need to connect to your instance.

After completing the instructions above, you're ready to proceed with the wizard to create an Auto Scaling group.

Create an Auto Scaling Group

Use the following procedure to continue where you left off after selecting or creating your launch configuration.

To create an Auto Scaling group

1. On the **Configure Auto Scaling group details** page, do the following:

   1. For **Group name**, type a name for your Auto Scaling group.

   2. For **Group size**, type the initial number of instances for your Auto Scaling group.

   3. If you selected an instance type for your launch configuration that requires a VPC, such as a T2 instance, you must select a VPC for **Network**. Otherwise, if your account supports EC2-Classic and you selected an instance type that doesn't require a VPC, you can select either `Launch into EC2-Classic` or a VPC.

   4. If you selected a VPC in the previous step, select one or more subnets from **Subnet**. If you selected EC2-Classic instead, select one or more Availability Zones from **Availability Zone(s)**.

   5. For **Advanced Details**, select `Receive traffic from Elastic Load Balancer(s)` and then do one of the following:
      - [Classic Load Balancers] Select your load balancer from **Load Balancers**.
      - [Target groups] Select your target group from **Target Groups**.

   6. (Optional) To use Elastic Load Balancing health checks, choose **ELB** for **Advanced Details, Health Check Type**.

   7. Choose **Next: Configure scaling policies**.

2. On the **Configure scaling policies** page, select **Keep this group at its initial size**, and then choose **Review**.

   If you want to configure scaling policies for your Auto Scaling group, see Create an Auto Scaling Group with Target Tracking Scaling Policies.

3. Review the details of your Auto Scaling group. You can choose **Edit** to make changes. When you are finished, choose **Create Auto Scaling group**.

(Optional) Verify that Your Load Balancer is Attached to Your Auto Scaling Group

To verify that your load balancer is attached to your Auto Scaling group

1. Select your Auto Scaling group.

2. On the **Details** tab, **Load Balancers** shows any attached load balancers and **Target Groups** shows any attached target groups.

3. On the **Details** tab, **Load Balancers** shows any attached load balancers.

4. On the **Activity History** tab, the **Status** column shows you the status of your Auto Scaling instances. While an instance is launching, its status is `In progress`. The status changes to `Successful` after the instance is launched.

5. On the **Instances** tab, the **Lifecycle** column shows the state of your Auto Scaling instances. After an instance is ready to receive traffic, its state is `InService`.

   The **Health Status** column shows the result of the health checks on your instances.

Configure Scaling and Load Balancing Using the AWS CLI

Complete the following tasks to set up a scaled and load-balanced application.

Topics

- Create a Launch Configuration
- Create an Auto Scaling Group with a Load Balancer

Create a Launch Configuration

If you already have a launch configuration that you'd like to use, skip this step.

To create the launch configuration
Use the following create-launch-configuration command:

```
1 aws autoscaling create-launch-configuration --launch-configuration-name my-lc \
2 --image-id ami-514ac838 --instance-type m1.small
```

Create an Auto Scaling Group with a Load Balancer

You can attach an existing load balancer to an Auto Scaling group when you create the group.

To create an Auto Scaling group with an attached Classic Load Balancer
Use the following create-auto-scaling-group command with the --load-balancer-names option to create an Auto Scaling group with an attached Classic Load Balancer:

```
1 aws autoscaling create-auto-scaling-group --auto-scaling-group-name my-lb-asg \
2 --launch-configuration-name my-lc \
3 --availability-zones "us-west-2a" "us-west-2b" \
4 --load-balancer-names "my-lb" \
5 --max-size 5 --min-size 1 --desired-capacity 2
```

To create an Auto Scaling group with an attached target group
Use the following create-auto-scaling-group command with the --target-group-arns option to create an Auto Scaling group with an attached target group:

```
1 aws autoscaling create-auto-scaling-group --auto-scaling-group-name my-lb-asg \
2 --launch-configuration-name my-lc \
3 --vpc-zone-identifier "subnet-41767929" \
4 --vpc-zone-identifier "subnet-b7d581c0" \
5 --target-group-arns "arn:aws:elasticloadbalancing:us-west-2:123456789012:targetgroup/my-targets
    /1234567890123456" \
6 --max-size 5 --min-size 1 --desired-capacity 2
```

Launch Configurations

A *launch configuration* is a template that an Auto Scaling group uses to launch EC2 instances. When you create a launch configuration, you specify information for the instances such as the ID of the Amazon Machine Image (AMI), the instance type, a key pair, one or more security groups, and a block device mapping. If you've launched an EC2 instance before, you specified the same information in order to launch the instance.

You can specify your launch configuration with multiple Auto Scaling groups. However, you can only specify one launch configuration for an Auto Scaling group at a time, and you can't modify a launch configuration after you've created it. Therefore, if you want to change the launch configuration for an Auto Scaling group, you must create a launch configuration and then update your Auto Scaling group with the new launch configuration.

Keep in mind that whenever you create an Auto Scaling group, you must specify a launch configuration, a launch template, or an EC2 instance. When you create an Auto Scaling group using an EC2 instance, Amazon EC2 Auto Scaling automatically creates a launch configuration for you and associates it with the Auto Scaling group. For more information, see Creating an Auto Scaling Group Using an EC2 Instance. Alternatively, if you create a launch template, you can use your launch template to create an Auto Scaling group instead of creating a launch configuration. For more information, see Creating an Auto Scaling Group Using a Launch Template.

Topics

- Creating a Launch Configuration
- Creating a Launch Configuration Using an EC2 Instance
- Changing the Launch Configuration for an Auto Scaling Group
- Copying a Launch Configuration to a Launch Template
- Replacing a Launch Configuration with a Launch Template
- Launching Auto Scaling Instances in a VPC

Creating a Launch Configuration

When you create a launch configuration, you must specify information about the EC2 instances to launch, such as the Amazon Machine Image (AMI), instance type, key pair, security groups, and block device mapping. Alternatively, you can create a launch configuration using attributes from a running EC2 instance. For more information, see Creating a Launch Configuration Using an EC2 Instance.

After you create a launch configuration, you can create an Auto Scaling group. For more information, see Creating an Auto Scaling Group Using a Launch Configuration.

An Auto Scaling group is associated with one launch configuration at a time, and you can't modify a launch configuration after you've created it. Therefore, if you want to change the launch configuration for an existing Auto Scaling group, you must update it with the new launch configuration. For more information, see Changing the Launch Configuration for an Auto Scaling Group.

To create a launch configuration using the console

1. Open the Amazon EC2 console at https://console.aws.amazon.com/ec2/.

2. On the navigation bar at the top of the screen, the current region is displayed. Select a region for your Auto Scaling group that meets your needs.

3. On the navigation pane, under **Auto Scaling**, choose **Launch Configurations**.

4. On the next page, choose **Create launch configuration**.

5. On the **Choose AMI** page, select an AMI.

6. On the **Choose Instance Type** page, select a hardware configuration for your instance. Choose **Next: Configure details**. **Note**
T2 instances must be launched into a subnet of a VPC. If you select a `t2.micro` instance but don't have a VPC, one is created for you. This VPC includes a public subnet in each Availability Zone in the region.

7. On the **Configure Details** page, do the following:

   1. For **Name**, type a name for your launch configuration.

   2. (Optional) For **IAM role**, select a role to associate with the instances. For more information, see Launch Auto Scaling Instances with an IAM Role.

   3. (Optional) By default, basic monitoring is enabled for your Auto Scaling instances. To enable detailed monitoring for your Auto Scaling instances, select **Enable CloudWatch detailed monitoring**.

   4. For **Advanced Details, IP Address Type**, select an option. To connect to instances in a VPC, you must select an option that assigns a public IP address. If you want to connect to your instances but aren't sure whether you have a default VPC, select **Assign a public IP address to every instance**.

   5. Choose **Skip to review**.

8. On the **Review** page, choose **Edit security groups**. Follow the instructions to choose an existing security group, and then choose **Review**.

9. On the **Review** page, choose **Create launch configuration**.

10. For **Select an existing key pair or create a new key pair**, select one of the listed options. Select the acknowledgment check box, and then choose **Create launch configuration**. **Warning**
Do not select **Proceed without a key pair** if you need to connect to your instance.

To create a launch configuration using the command line

You can use one of the following commands:

- create-launch-configuration (AWS CLI)

- New-ASLaunchConfiguration (AWS Tools for Windows PowerShell)

Creating a Launch Configuration Using an EC2 Instance

Amazon EC2 Auto Scaling provides you with an option to create a launch configuration using the attributes from a running EC2 instance.

Tip

You can create an Auto Scaling group directly from an EC2 instance. When you use this feature, Amazon EC2 Auto Scaling automatically creates a launch configuration for you as well.

If the specified instance has properties that are not currently supported by launch configurations, the instances launched by the Auto Scaling group might not be identical to the original EC2 instance.

There are differences between creating a launch configuration from scratch and creating a launch configuration from an existing EC2 instance. When you create a launch configuration from scratch, you specify the image ID, instance type, optional resources (such as storage devices), and optional settings (like monitoring). When you create a launch configuration from a running instance, Amazon EC2 Auto Scaling derives attributes for the launch configuration from the specified instance, plus the block device mapping for the AMI that the instance was launched from (ignoring any additional block devices that were added to the instance after launch).

When you create a launch configuration using a running instance, you can override the following attributes by specifying them as part of the same request: AMI, block devices, key pair, instance profile, instance type, kernel, monitoring, placement tenancy, ramdisk, security groups, Spot price, user data, whether the instance has a public IP address is associated, and whether the instance is EBS-optimized.

The following examples show you to create a launch configuration from an EC2 instance.

Topics

- Create a Launch Configuration Using an EC2 Instance
- Create a Launch Configuration from an Instance and Override the Block Devices
- Create a Launch Configuration and Override the Instance Type

Create a Launch Configuration Using an EC2 Instance

To create a launch configuration using the attributes of an existing EC2 instance, specify the ID of the instance.

Important

The AMI used to launch the specified instance must still exist.

Create a Launch Configuration from an EC2 Instance Using the AWS Management Console

You can use the console to create a launch configuration and an Auto Scaling group from a running EC2 instance and add the instance to the new Auto Scaling group. For more information, see Attach EC2 Instances to Your Auto Scaling Group.

Create a Launch Configuration from an EC2 Instance Using the AWS CLI

Use the following create-launch-configuration command to create a launch configuration from an instance using the same attributes as the instance (other than any block devices added after launch, which are ignored):

```
1 aws autoscaling create-launch-configuration --launch-configuration-name my-lc-from-instance --
    instance-id i-a8e09d9c
```

You can use the following describe-launch-configurations command to describe the launch configuration and verify that its attributes match those of the instance:

```
1 aws autoscaling describe-launch-configurations --launch-configuration-names my-lc-from-instance
```

The following is an example response:

```
1  {
2      "LaunchConfigurations": [
3          {
4              "UserData": null,
5              "EbsOptimized": false,
6              "LaunchConfigurationARN": "arn",
7              "InstanceMonitoring": {
8                  "Enabled": false
9              },
10             "ImageId": "ami-05355a6c",
11             "CreatedTime": "2014-12-29T16:14:50.382Z",
12             "BlockDeviceMappings": [],
13             "KeyName": "my-key-pair",
14             "SecurityGroups": [
15                 "sg-8422d1eb"
16             ],
17             "LaunchConfigurationName": "my-lc-from-instance",
18             "KernelId": "null",
19             "RamdiskId": null,
20             "InstanceType": "t1.micro",
21             "AssociatePublicIpAddress": true
22         }
23     ]
24 }
```

Create a Launch Configuration from an Instance and Override the Block Devices

By default, Amazon EC2 Auto Scaling uses the attributes from the EC2 instance you specify to create the launch configuration, except that the block devices come from the AMI used to launch the instance, not the instance. To add block devices to the launch configuration, override the block device mapping for the launch configuration.

Important
The AMI used to launch the specified instance must still exist.

Create a Launch Configuration and Override the Block Devices Using the AWS CLI

Use the following create-launch-configuration command to create a launch configuration using an EC2 instance but with a custom block device mapping:

```
1  aws autoscaling create-launch-configuration --launch-configuration-name my-lc-from-instance-bdm
      --instance-id i-a8e09d9c
2  --block-device-mappings "[{\"DeviceName\":\"/dev/sda1\",\"Ebs\":{\"SnapshotId\":\"snap-3decf207
      \"}},{\"DeviceName\":\"/dev/sdf\",\"Ebs\":{\"SnapshotId\":\"snap-eed6ac86\"}}]"
```

Use the following describe-launch-configurations command to describe the launch configuration and verify that it uses your custom block device mapping:

```
1  aws autoscaling describe-launch-configurations --launch-configuration-names my-lc-from-instance-
      bdm
```

The following example response describes the launch configuration:

```
 1  {
 2      "LaunchConfigurations": [
 3          {
 4              "UserData": null,
 5              "EbsOptimized": false,
 6              "LaunchConfigurationARN": "arn",
 7              "InstanceMonitoring": {
 8                  "Enabled": false
 9              },
10              "ImageId": "ami-c49c0dac",
11              "CreatedTime": "2015-01-07T14:51:26.065Z",
12              "BlockDeviceMappings": [
13                  {
14                      "DeviceName": "/dev/sda1",
15                      "Ebs": {
16                          "SnapshotId": "snap-3decf207"
17                      }
18                  },
19                  {
20                      "DeviceName": "/dev/sdf",
21                      "Ebs": {
22                          "SnapshotId": "snap-eed6ac86"
23                      }
24                  }
25              ],
26              "KeyName": "my-key-pair",
27              "SecurityGroups": [
28                  "sg-8637d3e3"
29              ],
30              "LaunchConfigurationName": "my-lc-from-instance-bdm",
31              "KernelId": null,
32              "RamdiskId": null,
33              "InstanceType": "t1.micro",
34              "AssociatePublicIpAddress": true
35          }
36      ]
37  }
```

Create a Launch Configuration and Override the Instance Type

By default, Amazon EC2 Auto Scaling uses the attributes from the EC2 instance you specify to create the launch configuration. Depending on your requirements, you might want to override attributes from the instance and use the values that you need. For example, you can override the instance type.

Important
The AMI used to launch the specified instance must still exist.

Create a Launch Configuration and Override the Instance Type Using the AWS CLI

Use the following create-launch-configuration command to create a launch configuration using an EC2 instance but with a different instance type (for example t2.medium) than the instance (for example t2.micro):

```
1 aws autoscaling create-launch-configuration --launch-configuration-name my-lc-from-instance-
    changetype --instance-id i-a8e09d9c --instance-type t2.medium
```

Use the following describe-launch-configurations command to describe the launch configuration and verify that the instance type was overridden:

```
1 aws autoscaling describe-launch-configurations --launch-configuration-names my-lc-from-instance-
    changetype
```

The following example response describes the launch configuration:

```
1  {
2      "LaunchConfigurations": [
3          {
4              "UserData": null,
5              "EbsOptimized": false,
6              "LaunchConfigurationARN": "arn",
7              "InstanceMonitoring": {
8                  "Enabled": false
9              },
10             "ImageId": "ami-05355a6c",
11             "CreatedTime": "2014-12-29T16:14:50.382Z",
12             "BlockDeviceMappings": [],
13             "KeyName": "my-key-pair",
14             "SecurityGroups": [
15                 "sg-8422d1eb"
16             ],
17             "LaunchConfigurationName": "my-lc-from-instance-changetype",
18             "KernelId": "null",
19             "RamdiskId": null,
20             "InstanceType": "t2.medium",
21             "AssociatePublicIpAddress": true
22         }
23     ]
24 }
```

Changing the Launch Configuration for an Auto Scaling Group

An Auto Scaling group is associated with one launch configuration at a time, and you can't modify a launch configuration after you've created it. To change the launch configuration for an Auto Scaling group, you can use an existing launch configuration as the basis for a new launch configuration and then update the Auto Scaling group to use the new launch configuration.

After you change the launch configuration for an Auto Scaling group, any new instances are launched using the new configuration options, but existing instances are not affected.

To change the launch configuration for an Auto Scaling group using the console

1. Open the Amazon EC2 console at https://console.aws.amazon.com/ec2/.

2. In the navigation pane, choose **Launch Configurations**.

3. Select the launch configuration and choose **Actions, Copy launch configuration**. This sets up a new launch configuration with the same options as the original, but with "Copy" added to the name.

4. On the **Copy Launch Configuration** page, edit the configuration options as needed and choose **Create launch configuration**.

5. On the confirmation page, choose **View your Auto Scaling groups**.

6. Select the Auto Scaling group and choose **Details, Edit**.

7. Select the new launch configuration from **Launch Configuration** and choose **Save**.

To change the launch configuration for an Auto Scaling group using the AWS CLI

1. Describe the current launch configuration using the describe-launch-configurations command.

2. Create a new launch configuration using the create-launch-configuration command.

3. Update the launch configuration for the Auto Scaling group using the update-auto-scaling-group command with the `--launch-configuration-names` parameter.

To change the launch configuration for an Auto Scaling group using the Tools for Windows PowerShell

1. Describe the current launch configuration using the Get-ASLaunchConfiguration command.

2. Create a new launch configuration using the New-ASLaunchConfiguration command.

3. Update the launch configuration for the Auto Scaling group using the Update-ASAutoScalingGroup command with the `-LaunchConfigurationName` parameter.

Copying a Launch Configuration to a Launch Template

Use the following procedure to copy the options from an existing launch configuration to create a new launch template.

You can create launch templates from existing launch configurations to make it easy for you to update your Auto Scaling groups to use launch templates. Like launch configurations, launch templates can contain all or some of the parameters to launch an instance. With launch templates, you can also create multiple versions of a template to make it faster and easier to launch new instances. For more information about using launch templates, see Launching an Instance from a Launch Template in the *Amazon EC2 User Guide for Linux Instances*.

To create a launch template from a launch configuration

1. Open the Amazon EC2 console at https://console.aws.amazon.com/ec2/.

2. In the navigation pane, choose **Launch Configurations**.

3. Select the launch configuration you want to copy and choose **Copy to launch template**. This sets up a new launch template with the same name and options as the launch configuration you selected.

4. For **New launch template name**, you can use the name of the launch configuration (the default) or type a new name. Note that launch template names must be unique.

5. (Optional) To create an Auto Scaling group using the new launch template, select **Create an Auto Scaling group using the new template**. For more information, see Creating an Auto Scaling Group Using a Launch Template.

6. Choose **Submit**.

After creating your launch template, you can update your existing Auto Scaling groups, as needed, with the launch template that you created. For more information, see Replacing a Launch Configuration with a Launch Template.

Replacing a Launch Configuration with a Launch Template

When you edit an Auto Scaling group that has an existing launch configuration, you have the option of replacing the launch configuration with a launch template. This lets you use launch templates with any Auto Scaling groups you currently use. In doing so, you can take advantage of the versioning features of launch templates.

After you replace the launch configuration for an Auto Scaling group, any new instances are launched using the new launch template, but existing instances are not affected.

Prerequisites
Before you can replace a launch configuration in an Auto Scaling group, you must first create your launch template. The easiest way to create a launch template is to copy it from the launch configuration. For more information, see Copying a Launch Configuration to a Launch Template.

To replace the launch configuration for an Auto Scaling group

1. Open the Amazon EC2 console at https://console.aws.amazon.com/ec2/.

2. In the navigation pane, choose **Auto Scaling Groups**.

3. Select the Auto Scaling group and choose **Details, Edit**.

4. For **Launch Instances Using**, choose the **Launch Template** option.

5. For **Launch Template**, select your launch template.

6. For **Launch Template Version**, select the launch template version, as needed. After you create versions of a launch template, you can choose whether the Auto Scaling group uses the default or the latest version of the launch template when scaling out.

7. When you have finished, choose **Save**.

Launching Auto Scaling Instances in a VPC

Amazon Virtual Private Cloud (Amazon VPC) enables you to define a virtual networking environment in a private, isolated section of the AWS cloud. You have complete control over your virtual networking environment. For more information, see the *Amazon VPC User Guide*.

Within a virtual private cloud (VPC), you can launch AWS resources such as an Auto Scaling group. An Auto Scaling group in a VPC works essentially the same way as it does on Amazon EC2 and supports the same set of features.

A subnet in Amazon VPC is a subdivision within an Availability Zone defined by a segment of the IP address range of the VPC. Using subnets, you can group your instances based on your security and operational needs. A subnet resides entirely within the Availability Zone it was created in. You launch Auto Scaling instances within the subnets.

To enable communication between the Internet and the instances in your subnets, you must create an Internet gateway and attach it to your VPC. An Internet gateway enables your resources within the subnets to connect to the Internet through the Amazon EC2 network edge. If a subnet's traffic is routed to an Internet gateway, the subnet is known as a *public* subnet. If a subnet's traffic is not routed to an Internet gateway, the subnet is known as a *private* subnet. Use a public subnet for resources that must be connected to the Internet, and a private subnet for resources that need not be connected to the Internet.

Prerequisites

Before you can launch your Auto Scaling instances in a VPC, you must first create your VPC environment. After you create your VPC and subnets, you launch Auto Scaling instances within the subnets. The easiest way to create a VPC with one public subnet is to use the VPC wizard. For more information, see the Amazon VPC Getting Started Guide.

Topics

- Default VPC
- IP Addressing in a VPC
- Instance Placement Tenancy
- Linking EC2-Classic Instances to a VPC
- Examples

Default VPC

If you have created your AWS account after 2013-12-04 or you are creating your Auto Scaling group in a new region, we create a default VPC for you. Your default VPC comes with a default subnet in each Availability Zone. If you have a default VPC, your Auto Scaling group is created in the default VPC by default.

For information about default VPCs and checking whether your account comes with a default VPC, see Your Default VPC and Subnets in the *Amazon VPC Developer Guide*.

IP Addressing in a VPC

When you launch your Auto Scaling instances in a VPC, your instances are automatically assigned a private IP address in the address range of the subnet. This enables your instances to communicate with other instances in the VPC.

You can configure your launch configuration to assign public IP addresses to your instances. Assigning public IP addresses to your instances enables them to communicate with the Internet or other services in AWS.

When you enable public IP addresses for your instances, they receive both IPv4 and IPv6 addresses if you launch them into a subnet that is configured to automatically assign IPv6 addresses to instances. Otherwise, they receive IPv4 addresses. For more information, see IPv6 Addresses in the *Amazon EC2 User Guide for Linux Instances*.

Instance Placement Tenancy

Dedicated Instances are physically isolated at the host hardware level from instances that aren't dedicated and from instances that belong to other AWS accounts. When you create a VPC, by default its tenancy attribute is set to `default`. In such a VPC, you can launch instances with a tenancy value of `dedicated` so that they run as single-tenancy instances. Otherwise, they run as shared-tenancy instances by default. If you set the tenancy attribute of a VPC to `dedicated`, all instances launched in the VPC run as single-tenancy instances. For more information, see Dedicated Instances in the *Amazon VPC User Guide*. For pricing information, see the Amazon EC2 Dedicated Instances product page.

When you create a launch configuration, the default value for the instance placement tenancy is `null` and the instance tenancy is controlled by the tenancy attribute of the VPC. The following table summarizes the instance placement tenancy of the Auto Scaling instances launched in a VPC.

Launch Configuration Tenancy	VPC Tenancy = default	VPC Tenancy = dedicated
not specified	shared-tenancy instance	Dedicated Instance
default	shared-tenancy instance	Dedicated Instance
dedicated	Dedicated Instance	Dedicated Instance

You can specify the instance placement tenancy for your launch configuration as `default` or `dedicated` using the create-launch-configuration command with the `--placement-tenancy` option. For example, the following command sets the launch configuration tenancy to `dedicated`:

```
1 aws autoscaling create-launch-configuration --launch-configuration-name my-launch-config --
      placement-tenancy dedicated --image-id ...
```

You can use the following describe-launch-configurations command to verify the instance placement tenancy of the launch configuration:

```
1 aws autoscaling describe-launch-configurations --launch-configuration-names my-launch-config
```

The following is example output for a launch configuration that creates Dedicated Instances. Note that `PlacementTenancy` is not part of the output for this command unless you have explicitly set the instance placement tenancy.

```
1  {
2      "LaunchConfigurations": [
3          {
4              "UserData": null,
5              "EbsOptimized": false,
6              "PlacementTenancy": "dedicated",
7              "LaunchConfigurationARN": "arn",
8              "InstanceMonitoring": {
9                  "Enabled": true
10             },
11             "ImageId": "ami-b5a7ea85",
12             "CreatedTime": "2015-03-08T23:39:49.011Z",
13             "BlockDeviceMappings": [],
14             "KeyName": null,
15             "SecurityGroups": [],
```

```
16          "LaunchConfigurationName": "my-launch-config",
17          "KernelId": null,
18          "RamdiskId": null,
19          "InstanceType": "m3.medium"
20      }
21  ]
```

Linking EC2-Classic Instances to a VPC

If you are launching the instances in your Auto Scaling group in EC2-Classic, you can link them to a VPC using *ClassicLink*. ClassicLink enables you to associate one or more security groups for the VPC with the EC2-Classic instances in your Auto Scaling group, enabling communication between these linked EC2-Classic instances and instances in the VPC using private IP addresses. For more information, see ClassicLink in the *Amazon EC2 User Guide for Linux Instances*.

If you have running EC2-Classic instances in your Auto Scaling group, you can link them to a VPC with ClassicLink enabled. For more information, see Linking an Instance to a VPC in the *Amazon EC2 User Guide for Linux Instances*. Alternatively, you can update the Auto Scaling group to use a launch configuration that automatically links the EC2-Classic instances to a VPC at launch, then terminate the running instances and let the Auto Scaling group launch new instances that are linked to the VPC.

Link to a VPC Using the AWS Management Console

Use the following procedure to create a launch configuration that links EC2-Classic instances to the specified VPC and update an existing Auto Scaling group to use the launch configuration.

To link EC2-Classic instances in an Auto Scaling group to a VPC using the console

1. Verify that the VPC has ClassicLink enabled. For more information, see Viewing Your ClassicLink-Enabled VPCs in the *Amazon EC2 User Guide for Linux Instances*.

2. Create a security group for the VPC that you are going to link EC2-Classic instances to, with rules to control communication between the linked EC2-Classic instances and instances in the VPC.

3. Open the Amazon EC2 console at https://console.aws.amazon.com/ec2/.

4. On the navigation pane, choose **Launch Configurations**.

5. Choose **Create launch configuration**.

6. On the **Choose AMI** page, select an AMI.

7. On the **Choose an Instance Type** page, select an instance type, and then choose **Next: Configure details**.

8. On the **Configure details** page, do the following:

   1. Type a name for your launch configuration.

   2. Expand **Advanced Details**, select the **IP Address Type** that you need, and then select **Link to VPC**.

   3. For **VPC**, select the VPC with ClassicLink enabled from step 1.

   4. For **Security Groups**, select the security group from step 2.

   5. Choose **Skip to review**.

9. On the **Review** page, make any changes that you need, and then choose **Create launch configuration**. For **Select an existing key pair or create a new key pair**, select an option, select the acknowledgment check box (if present), and then choose **Create launch configuration**.

10. When prompted, follow the directions to create an Auto Scaling group that uses the new launch configuration. Be sure to select **Launch into EC2-Classic** for **Network**. Otherwise, choose **Cancel** and then add your launch configuration to an existing Auto Scaling group as follows:

    1. On the navigation pane, choose **Auto Scaling Groups**.

    2. Select your Auto Scaling group, choose **Actions**, **Edit**.

    3. For **Launch Configuration**, select your new launch configuration and then choose **Save**.

Link to a VPC Using the AWS CLI

Use the following procedure to create a launch configuration that links EC2-Classic instances to the specified VPC and update an existing Auto Scaling group to use the launch configuration.

To link EC2-Classic instances in an Auto Scaling group to a VPC using the AWS CLI

1. Verify that the VPC has ClassicLink enabled. For more information, see Viewing Your ClassicLink-Enabled VPCs in the *Amazon EC2 User Guide for Linux Instances*.

2. Create a security group for the VPC that you are going to link EC2-Classic instances to, with rules to control communication between the linked EC2-Classic instances and instances in the VPC.

3. Create a launch configuration using the create-launch-configuration command as follows, where *vpd_id* is the ID of the VPC with ClassicLink enabled from step 1 and *group_id* is the security group from step 2:

```
1 aws autoscaling create-launch-configuration --launch-configuration-name classiclink-config
2 --image-id ami_id --instance-type instance_type
3 --classic-link-vpc-id vpc_id --classic-link-vpc-security-groups group_id
```

4. Update your existing Auto Scaling group, for example *my-asg*, with the launch configuration that you created in the previous step. Any new EC2-Classic instances launched in this Auto Scaling group are linked EC2-Classic instances. Use the update-auto-scaling-group command as follows:

```
1 aws autoscaling update-auto-scaling-group --auto-scaling-group-name my-asg
2 --launch-configuration-name classiclink-config
```

   Alternatively, you can use this launch configuration with a new Auto Scaling group that you create using create-auto-scaling-group.

Examples

For examples, see the following tutorials:

- Getting Started with Amazon EC2 Auto Scaling
- Hosting a Web App on Amazon Web Services
- Hosting a .NET Web App on Amazon Web Services

Auto Scaling Groups

An *Auto Scaling group* contains a collection of EC2 instances that share similar characteristics and are treated as a logical grouping for the purposes of instance scaling and management. For example, if a single application operates across multiple instances, you might want to increase the number of instances in that group to improve the performance of the application, or decrease the number of instances to reduce costs when demand is low. You can use the Auto Scaling group to scale the number of instances automatically based on criteria that you specify, or maintain a fixed number of instances even if an instance becomes unhealthy. This automatic scaling and maintaining the number of instances in an Auto Scaling group is the core functionality of the Amazon EC2 Auto Scaling service.

An Auto Scaling group starts by launching enough EC2 instances to meet its desired capacity. The Auto Scaling group maintains this number of instances by performing periodic health checks on the instances in the group. If an instance becomes unhealthy, the group terminates the unhealthy instance and launches another instance to replace it. For more information about health check replacements, see Maintaining the Number of Instances in Your Auto Scaling Group.

You can use scaling policies to increase or decrease the number of running EC2 instances in your group automatically to meet changing conditions. When the scaling policy is in effect, the Auto Scaling group adjusts the desired capacity of the group and launches or terminates the instances as needed. If you manually scale or scale on a schedule, you must adjust the desired capacity of the group in order for the changes to take effect. For more information, see Scaling the Size of Your Auto Scaling Group.

Before you get started, take the time to review your application thoroughly as it runs in the AWS cloud. Take note of the following:

- How long it takes to launch and configure a server
- What metrics have the most relevance to your application's performance
- How many Availability Zones you want the Auto Scaling group to span
- Do you want to scale to increase or decrease capacity? Do you just want to ensure that a specific number of servers are always running? (Keep in mind that Amazon EC2 Auto Scaling can do both simultaneously.)
- What existing resources (such as EC2 instances or AMIs) you can use

The better you understand your application, the more effective you can make your Auto Scaling architecture.

Topics

- Creating an Auto Scaling Group Using a Launch Template
- Creating an Auto Scaling Group Using a Launch Configuration
- Creating an Auto Scaling Group Using an EC2 Instance
- Creating an Auto Scaling Group Using the Amazon EC2 Launch Wizard
- Tagging Auto Scaling Groups and Instances
- Using a Load Balancer With an Auto Scaling Group
- Launching Spot Instances in Your Auto Scaling Group
- Merging Your Auto Scaling Groups into a Single Multi-Zone Group
- Deleting Your Auto Scaling Infrastructure

Creating an Auto Scaling Group Using a Launch Template

When you create an Auto Scaling group, you must specify the information needed to configure the Auto Scaling instances and the minimum number of instances your group must maintain at all times.

When you create an Auto Scaling group using a launch template, you specify which version of the launch template the Auto Scaling group uses to launch Auto Scaling instances. You can specify a specific version (using the API, AWS CLI, or an SDK, but not the console). Alternatively, you can configure the Auto Scaling group to select either the default version or the latest version of the launch template dynamically when a scale out event occurs.

If you configured your Auto Scaling group to select either the default version or the latest version of a launch template dynamically, you can change the configuration of the Auto Scaling instances to be launched by the group by creating a new version or new default version of the launch template.

With the API, AWS CLI, or an SDK, when you update your Auto Scaling group, you can specify a different launch template for the group. You can also specify a launch template when you update an Auto Scaling group that was created using a launch configuration.

The following procedure demonstrates how to create an Auto Scaling group using a launch template.

Prerequisites

- Create a launch template. You must ensure that your template includes all parameters required to launch an EC2 instance, such as an AMI ID and an instance type. Otherwise, when you use the template to create an Auto Scaling group, you receive an error that you must use a fully-formed launch template. For more information, see Launching an Instance from a Launch Template in the *Amazon EC2 User Guide for Linux Instances*.
- An IAM user or role that creates an Auto Scaling group using a launch template must have permission to use the ec2:RunInstances action and permission to create or use the resources for the instance. For example, access to the iam:PassRole action is required to use an instance profile. You can use the **AmazonEC2FullAccess** policy to grant full access to all Amazon EC2 resources. You can use resource-level permissions to restrict access to specific launch templates. For more information, see Require a Launch Template or Launch Templates in the *Amazon EC2 User Guide for Linux Instances*.

Limitations

The following are limitations when creating a launch template for use with an Auto Scaling group:

- You cannot specify multiple network interfaces.
- If you specify a network interface, its device index must be 0.
- If you specify a network interface, you must specify any security groups as part of the network interface.
- You cannot specify private IP addresses.
- You cannot use host placement affinity.
- If you specify Spot Instances, you must specify a one-time request with no end date.

To create an Auto Scaling group using a launch template

1. Open the Amazon EC2 console at https://console.aws.amazon.com/ec2/.

2. On the navigation bar at the top of the screen, select the same region that you used when you created the launch template.

3. In the navigation pane, choose **Auto Scaling Groups**.

4. Choose **Create Auto Scaling group**.

5. Choose **Launch Template**, select your launch template, and then choose **Next Step**.

6. On the **Configure Auto Scaling group details** page, do the following:

   1. For **Launch template version**, choose whether the Auto Scaling group uses the default or the latest version of the launch template when scaling out.

2. For **Group name**, type a name for your Auto Scaling group.

3. For **Group size**, type the initial number of instances for your Auto Scaling group.

4. (Optional) To override the network in the launch template, select a VPC for **Network**.

5. (Optional) To override the network in the launch template, select one or more subnets for **Subnet**.

6. (Optional) To register your Auto Scaling instances with a load balancer, select **Receive traffic from one or more load balancers** and select one or more Classic Load Balancers or target groups.

7. Choose **Next: Configure scaling policies**.

7. On the **Configure scaling policies** page, select one of the following options, and then choose **Next: Configure Notifications**:

   - To manually adjust the size of the Auto Scaling group as needed, select **Keep this group at its initial size**. For more information, see Manual Scaling.
   - To automatically adjust the size of the Auto Scaling group based on criteria that you specify, select **Use scaling policies to adjust the capacity of this group** and follow the directions. For more information, see Configure Scaling Policies.

8. (Optional) To receive notifications, choose **Add notification**, configure the notification, and then choose **Next: Configure Tags**.

9. (Optional) To add tags, choose **Edit tags**, provide a tag key and value for each tag, and then choose **Review**.

   Alternatively, you can add tags later on. For more information, see Tagging Auto Scaling Groups and Instances.

10. On the **Review** page, choose **Create Auto Scaling group**.

11. On the **Auto Scaling group creation status** page, choose **Close**.

To create an Auto Scaling group using the command line

You can use one of the following commands:

   - create-auto-scaling-group (AWS CLI)
   - New-ASAutoScalingGroup (AWS Tools for Windows PowerShell)

Creating an Auto Scaling Group Using a Launch Configuration

When you create an Auto Scaling group, you must specify the information needed to configure the Auto Scaling instances and the minimum number of instances your group must maintain at all times.

The following procedures demonstrate how to create an Auto Scaling group using a launch configuration. You cannot modify a launch configuration after it is created, but you can replace the launch configuration for an Auto Scaling group. For more information, see Changing the Launch Configuration for an Auto Scaling Group.

Prerequisites
Create a launch configuration. For more information, see Creating a Launch Configuration.

To create an Auto Scaling group using the console

1. Open the Amazon EC2 console at https://console.aws.amazon.com/ec2/.

2. On the navigation bar at the top of the screen, select the same region that you used when you created the launch configuration.

3. On the navigation pane, under **Auto Scaling**, choose **Auto Scaling Groups**.

4. Choose **Create Auto Scaling group**.

5. On the **Create Auto Scaling Group** page, choose **Launch Configuration**, select an existing launch configuration, and then choose **Next Step**. **Note**
If you do not have any launch configurations, you're first prompted to create one before you can continue with the steps to create an Auto Scaling group.

6. On the **Configure Auto Scaling group details** page, do the following:

    1. For **Group name**, type a name for your Auto Scaling group.

    2. For **Group size**, type the initial number of instances for your Auto Scaling group.

    3. For **Network**, select a VPC for your Auto Scaling group.

    4. For **Subnet**, select one or more subnets.

    5. (Optional) To register your Auto Scaling instances with a load balancer, select **Receive traffic from one or more load balancers** and select one or more Classic Load Balancers or target groups.

    6. Choose **Next: Configure scaling policies**.

7. On the **Configure scaling policies** page, select one of the following options, and then choose **Next: Configure Notifications**:

    - To manually adjust the size of the Auto Scaling group as needed, select **Keep this group at its initial size**. For more information, see Manual Scaling.
    - To automatically adjust the size of the Auto Scaling group based on criteria that you specify, select **Use scaling policies to adjust the capacity of this group** and follow the directions. For more information, see Configure Scaling Policies.

8. (Optional) To receive notifications, choose **Add notification**, configure the notification, and then choose **Next: Configure Tags**.

9. (Optional) To add tags, choose **Edit tags**, provide a tag key and value for each tag, and then choose **Review**.

    Alternatively, you can add tags later on. For more information, see Tagging Auto Scaling Groups and Instances.

10. On the **Review** page, choose **Create Auto Scaling group**.

11. On the **Auto Scaling group creation status** page, choose **Close**.

To create an Auto Scaling group using the command line

You can use one of the following commands:

- create-auto-scaling-group (AWS CLI)
- New-ASAutoScalingGroup (AWS Tools for Windows PowerShell)

Creating an Auto Scaling Group Using an EC2 Instance

When you create an Auto Scaling group, you must specify the information needed to configure the Auto Scaling instances and the minimum number of instances your group must maintain at all times.

To configure Auto Scaling instances, you can specify a launch configuration, a launch template, or an EC2 instance. The following procedure demonstrates how to create an Auto Scaling group using an EC2 instance. To use a launch configuration or a launch template, see Creating an Auto Scaling Group Using a Launch Configuration or Creating an Auto Scaling Group Using a Launch Template.

When you create an Auto Scaling group using an EC2 instance, Amazon EC2 Auto Scaling automatically creates a launch configuration for you and associates it with the Auto Scaling group. This launch configuration has the same name as the Auto Scaling group, and it derives its attributes, such as AMI ID, instance type, and Availability Zone, from the specified instance.

Limitations
The following are limitations when creating an Auto Scaling group from an EC2 instance:

- If the identified instance has tags, the tags are not copied to the `Tags` attribute of the new Auto Scaling group.
- The Auto Scaling group includes the block device mapping from the AMI used to launch the instance; it does not include any block devices attached after instance launch.
- If the identified instance is registered with one or more load balancers, the load balancer names are not copied to the `LoadBalancerNames` attribute of the new Auto Scaling group.

Prerequisites

Before you begin, find the ID of the EC2 instance using the Amazon EC2 console or the describe-instances command (AWS CLI). The EC2 instance must meet the following criteria:

- The instance is in the Availability Zone in which you want to create the Auto Scaling group.
- The instance is not a member of another Auto Scaling group.
- The instance is in `running` state.
- The AMI used to launch the instance must still exist.

Topics

- Create an Auto Scaling Group from an EC2 Instance Using the Console
- Create an Auto Scaling Group from an EC2 Instance Using the AWS CLI

Create an Auto Scaling Group from an EC2 Instance Using the Console

You can use the console to create an Auto Scaling group from a running EC2 instance and add the instance to the new Auto Scaling group. For more information, see Attach EC2 Instances to Your Auto Scaling Group.

Create an Auto Scaling Group from an EC2 Instance Using the AWS CLI

Use the following create-auto-scaling-group command to create an Auto Scaling group, *my-asg-from-instance*, from the EC2 instance `i-7f12e649`.

```
1 aws autoscaling create-auto-scaling-group --auto-scaling-group-name my-asg-from-instance --
      instance-id i-7f12e649 --min-size 1 --max-size 2 --desired-capacity 2
```

Use the following describe-auto-scaling-groups command to create the Auto Scaling group.

```
1 aws autoscaling describe-auto-scaling-groups --auto-scaling-group-name my-asg-from-instance
```

The following example response shows that the desired capacity of the group is 2, the group has 2 running instances, and the launch configuration is also named *my-asg-from-instance*:

```
1  {
2      "AutoScalingGroups": [
3          {
4              "AutoScalingGroupARN": "arn",
5              "HealthCheckGracePeriod": 0,
6              "SuspendedProcesses": [],
7              "DesiredCapacity": 2,
8              "Tags": [],
9              "EnabledMetrics": [],
10             "LoadBalancerNames": [],
11             "AutoScalingGroupName": "my-asg-from-instance",
12             "DefaultCooldown": 300,
13             "MinSize": 1,
14             "Instances": [
15                 {
16                     "InstanceId": "i-6bd79d87",
17                     "AvailabilityZone": "us-west-2a",
18                     "HealthStatus": "Healthy",
19                     "LifecycleState": "InService",
20                     "LaunchConfigurationName": "my-asg-from-instance"
21                 },
22                 {
23                     "InstanceId": "i-6cd79d80",
24                     "AvailabilityZone": "us-west-2a",
25                     "HealthStatus": "Healthy",
26                     "LifecycleState": "InService",
27                     "LaunchConfigurationName": "my-asg-from-instance"
28                 }
29             ],
30             "MaxSize": 2,
31             "VPCZoneIdentifier": "subnet-6bea5f06",
32             "TerminationPolicies": [
33                 "Default"
34             ],
35             "LaunchConfigurationName": "my-asg-from-instance",
36             "CreatedTime": "2014-12-29T16:14:50.397Z",
37             "AvailabilityZones": [
38                 "us-west-2a"
39             ],
40             "HealthCheckType": "EC2"
41         }
42     ]
43 }
```

Use the following `describe-launch-configs` command to describe the launch configuration *my-asg-from-instance*.

```
1 aws autoscaling describe-launch-configurations --launch-configuration-names my-asg-from-instance
```

Creating an Auto Scaling Group Using the Amazon EC2 Launch Wizard

You can create a launch configuration and an Auto Scaling group in a single procedure by using the Amazon EC2 launch wizard. This is useful if you're launching more than one instance, and want to create a new launch configuration and Auto Scaling group from settings you've already selected in the Amazon EC2 launch wizard. You cannot use this option to create an Auto Scaling group using an existing launch configuration.

To create a launch configuration and Auto Scaling group using the launch wizard

1. Open the Amazon EC2 console at https://console.aws.amazon.com/ec2/.

2. From the dashboard, choose **Launch Instance**.

3. Choose an AMI, then choose an instance type on the next page, and then choose **Next: Configure Instance Details**.

4. In **Number of instances**, enter the number of instances that you want to launch, and then choose **Launch into Auto Scaling Group**. You do not need to enter any other configuration details on the page.

5. On the confirmation page, choose **Create Launch Configuration**.

6. You are switched to step 3 of the launch configuration wizard. The AMI and instance type are already selected based on the selection you made in the Amazon EC2 launch wizard. Enter a name for the launch configuration, configure any other settings as required, and then choose **Next: Add Storage**.

7. Configure any additional volumes, and then choose **Next: Configure Security Group**.

8. Create a new security group, or choose an existing group, and then choose **Review**.

9. Review the details of the launch configuration, and then choose **Create launch configuration** to choose a key pair and create the launch configuration.

10. On the **Configure Auto Scaling group details** page, the launch configuration you created is already selected for you, and the number of instances you specified in the Amazon EC2 launch wizard is populated for **Group size**. Enter a name for the group, specify a VPC and subnet (if required), and then choose **Next: Configure scaling policies**.

11. On the **Configure scaling policies** page, choose one of the following options, and then choose **Review**:

    - To manually adjust the size of the Auto Scaling group as needed, select **Keep this group at its initial size**. For more information, see Manual Scaling.
    - To automatically adjust the size of the Auto Scaling group based on criteria that you specify, select **Use scaling policies to adjust the capacity of this group** and follow the directions. For more information, see Configure Scaling Policies.

12. On the **Review** page, you can optionally add tags or notifications, and edit other configuration details. When you have finished, choose **Create Auto Scaling group**.

Tagging Auto Scaling Groups and Instances

You can organize and manage your Auto Scaling groups by assigning your own metadata to each group in the form of *tags*. You specify a *key* and a *value* for each tag. A key can be a general category, such as "project", "owner", or "environment", with specific associated values. For example, to differentiate between your testing and production environments, you could assign each Auto Scaling group a tag with a key of "environment", and either a value of "test" to indicate your test environment or "production" to indicate your production environment. We recommend that you use a consistent set of tags to make it easier to track your Auto Scaling groups.

You can specify that the tags for your Auto Scaling group should be added to the EC2 instances that it launches. The Auto Scaling group applies the tags while the instances are in the `Pending` lifecycle state. If you have a lifecycle hook, the tags are available when the instance enters the `Pending:Wait` lifecycle state. For more information, see Auto Scaling Lifecycle.

Tagging your EC2 instances enables you to see instance cost allocation by tag in your AWS bill. For more information, see Using Cost Allocation Tags in the *AWS Billing and Cost Management User Guide*.

Topics

- Tag Restrictions
- Tagging Lifecycle
- Add or Modify Tags for Your Auto Scaling Group
- Delete Tags

Tag Restrictions

The following basic restrictions apply to tags:

- The maximum number of tags per resource is 50.
- The maximum number of tags that you can add or remove using a single call is 25.
- The maximum key length is 127 Unicode characters.
- The maximum value length is 255 Unicode characters.
- Tag keys and values are case sensitive.
- Do not use the `aws:` prefix in your tag names or values, because it is reserved for AWS use. You can't edit or delete tag names or values with this prefix, and they do not count against toward your limit of tags per Auto Scaling group.

You can add tags to your Auto Scaling group when you create it or when you update it. You can remove tags from your Auto Scaling group at any time. For information about assigning tags when you create your Auto Scaling group, see Step 2: Create an Auto Scaling Group.

Tagging Lifecycle

If you have opted to propagate tags to your Auto Scaling instances, the tags are managed as follows:

- When an Auto Scaling group launches instances, it adds the tags to the instances. In addition, it adds a tag with a key of `aws:autoscaling:groupName` and a value of the name of the Auto Scaling group.
- When you attach existing instances, the Auto Scaling group adds the tags to the instances, overwriting any existing tags with the same tag key. In addition, it adds a tag with a key of `aws:autoscaling:groupName` and a value of the name of the Auto Scaling group.
- When you detach an instance from an Auto Scaling group, it removes only the `aws:autoscaling:groupName` tag.
- When you scale in manually or the Auto Scaling group automatically scales in, it removes all tags from the instances that are terminating.

Add or Modify Tags for Your Auto Scaling Group

When you add a tag to your Auto Scaling group, you can specify whether it should be added to instances launched in the Auto Scaling group. If you modify a tag, the updated version of the tag is added to instances launched in the Auto Scaling group after the change. If you create or modify a tag for an Auto Scaling group, these changes are not made to instances that are already running in the Auto Scaling group.

Topics

- Add or Modify Tags Using the AWS Management Console
- Add or Modify Tags Using the AWS CLI

Add or Modify Tags Using the AWS Management Console

Use the Amazon EC2 console to add or modify tags.

To add or modify tags

1. Open the Amazon EC2 console at https://console.aws.amazon.com/ec2/.

2. On the navigation pane, under **Auto Scaling**, choose **Auto Scaling Groups**.

3. Select your Auto Scaling group.

4. On the **Tags** tab, choose **Add/Edit tags**. The **Add/Edit Auto Scaling Group Tags** page lists any existing tags for the Auto Scaling group.

5. To modify existing tags, edit **Key** and **Value**.

6. To add a new tag, choose **Add tag** and edit **Key** and **Value**. You can keep **Tag New Instances** selected to add the tag to the instances launched in the Auto Scaling group automatically, and deselect it otherwise.

7. When you have finished adding tags, choose **Save**.

Add or Modify Tags Using the AWS CLI

Use the create-or-update-tags command to create or modify a tag. For example, the following command adds a tag with a key of "environment" and a value of "test" that will also be added to instances launched in the Auto Scaling group after this change. If a tag with this key already exists, the existing tag is replaced.

```
1 aws autoscaling create-or-update-tags --tags "ResourceId=my-asg,ResourceType=auto-scaling-group,
    Key=environment,Value=test,PropagateAtLaunch=true"
```

The following is an example response:

```
1 OK-Created/Updated tags
```

Use the following describe-tags command to list the tags for the specified Auto Scaling group.

```
1 aws autoscaling describe-tags --filters Name=auto-scaling-group,Values=my-asg
```

The following is an example response:

```
1 {
2     "Tags": [
3         {
4             "ResourceType": "auto-scaling-group",
5             "ResourceId": "my-asg",
6             "PropagateAtLaunch": true,
7             "Value": "test",
```

```
 8            "Key": "environment"
 9        }
10    ]
11 }
```

Alternatively, use the following describe-auto-scaling-groups command to verify that the tag is added to the Auto Scaling group.

```
1 aws autoscaling describe-auto-scaling-groups --auto-scaling-group-name my-asg
```

The following is an example response:

```
 1 {
 2     "AutoScalingGroups": [
 3         {
 4             "AutoScalingGroupARN": "arn",
 5             "HealthCheckGracePeriod": 0,
 6             "SuspendedProcesses": [],
 7             "DesiredCapacity": 1,
 8             "Tags": [
 9                 {
10                     "ResourceType": "auto-scaling-group",
11                     "ResourceId": "my-asg",
12                     "PropagateAtLaunch": true,
13                     "Value": "test",
14                     "Key": "environment"
15                 }
16             ],
17             "EnabledMetrics": [],
18             "LoadBalancerNames": [],
19             "AutoScalingGroupName": "my-asg",
20             ...
21         }
22     ]
23 }
```

Delete Tags

You can delete a tag associated with your Auto Scaling group at any time.

Topics

- Delete Tags Using the AWS Management Console
- Delete Tags Using the AWS CLI

Delete Tags Using the AWS Management Console

To delete a tag using the console

1. Open the Amazon EC2 console at https://console.aws.amazon.com/ec2/.

2. On the navigation pane, under **Auto Scaling**, choose **Auto Scaling Groups**.

3. Select your Auto Scaling group.

4. On the **Tags** tab, choose **Add/Edit tags**. The **Add/Edit Auto Scaling Group Tags** page lists any existing tags for the Auto Scaling group.

5. Choose the delete icon next to the tag.

6. Choose **Save**.

Delete Tags Using the AWS CLI

Use the delete-tags command to delete a tag. For example, the following command deletes a tag with a key of "environment".

```
1 aws autoscaling delete-tags --tags "ResourceId=my-asg,ResourceType=auto-scaling-group,Key=
    environment"
```

Notice that you must specify the tag key, but you don't need to specify the value. If you specify a value and the value is incorrect, the tag is not deleted.

Using a Load Balancer With an Auto Scaling Group

You can automatically increase the size of your Auto Scaling group when demand goes up and decrease it when demand goes down. As the Auto Scaling group adds and removes EC2 instances, you must ensure that the traffic for your application is distributed across all of your EC2 instances. The Elastic Load Balancing service automatically routes incoming web traffic across such a dynamically changing number of EC2 instances. Your load balancer acts as a single point of contact for all incoming traffic to the instances in your Auto Scaling group. For more information, see the Elastic Load Balancing User Guide.

To use a load balancer with your Auto Scaling group, create the load balancer and then attach it to the group.

Topics

- Attaching a Load Balancer to Your Auto Scaling Group
- Using ELB Health Checks with Auto Scaling
- Expanding Your Scaled and Load-Balanced Application to an Additional Availability Zone

Attaching a Load Balancer to Your Auto Scaling Group

Amazon EC2 Auto Scaling integrates with Elastic Load Balancing to enable you to attach one or more load balancers to an existing Auto Scaling group. After you attach the load balancer, it automatically registers the instances in the group and distributes incoming traffic across the instances. To use an Elastic Load Balancing health check with your instances to ensure that traffic is routed only to the healthy instances, see Using ELB Health Checks with Auto Scaling.

When you attach a load balancer, it enters the `Adding` state while registering the instances in the group. After all instances in the group are registered with the load balancer, it enters the `Added` state. After at least one registered instance passes the health checks, it enters the `InService` state. After the load balancer enters the `InService` state, Amazon EC2 Auto Scaling can terminate and replace any instances that are reported as unhealthy. Note that if no registered instances pass the health checks (for example, due to a misconfigured health check), the load balancer doesn't enter the `InService` state, so Amazon EC2 Auto Scaling wouldn't terminate and replace the instances.

When you detach a load balancer, it enters the `Removing` state while deregistering the instances in the group. Note that the instances remain running after they are deregistered. If connection draining is enabled, Elastic Load Balancing waits for in-flight requests to complete or for the maximum timeout to expire (whichever comes first) before deregistering the instances. Note that connection draining is always enabled for Application Load Balancers but must be enabled for Classic Load Balancers. For more information, see Connection Draining in the *User Guide for Classic Load Balancers.*

Elastic Load Balancing sends data about your load balancers and EC2 instances to Amazon CloudWatch. CloudWatch collects performance data for your resources and presents it as metrics. For more information, see Monitoring Your Auto Scaling Groups and Instances Using Amazon CloudWatch. After you attach a load balancer to your Auto Scaling group, you can create scaling policies that use Elastic Load Balancing metrics to scale your application automatically. For more information, see Create an Auto Scaling Group with Target Tracking Scaling Policies.

Topics

- Prerequisites
- Add a Load Balancer Using the Console
- Add a Load Balancer Using the AWS CLI

Prerequisites

Before you begin, create a load balancer in the same region as the Auto Scaling group. Elastic Load Balancing supports three types of load balancers: Application Load Balancers, Network Load Balancers, and Classic Load Balancers. You can attach any of these types of load balancers to your Auto Scaling group. For more information, see the Elastic Load Balancing User Guide.

With Classic Load Balancers, instances are registered with the load balancer. With Application Load Balancers and Network Load Balancers, instances are registered as targets with a target group. When you plan to use your load balancer with an Auto Scaling group, you don't need to register your EC2 instances with the load balancer or target group. After you attach a load balancer or target group to your Auto Scaling group, the Auto Scaling group registers your instances with the load balancer or target group when it launches them.

Add a Load Balancer Using the Console

Use the following procedure to attach a load balancer to an existing Auto Scaling group. To attach your load balancer to your Auto Scaling group when you create the Auto Scaling group, see Tutorial: Set Up a Scaled and Load-Balanced Application.

To attach a load balancer to a group

1. Open the Amazon EC2 console at https://console.aws.amazon.com/ec2/.

2. On the navigation pane, under **Auto Scaling**, choose **Auto Scaling Groups**.

3. Select your group.

4. On the **Details** tab, choose **Edit**.

5. Do one of the following:

    1. [Classic Load Balancers] For **Load Balancers**, select your load balancer.

    2. [Target groups] For **Target Groups**, select your target group.

6. Choose **Save**.

When you no longer need the load balancer, use the following procedure to detach it from your Auto Scaling group.

To detach a load balancer from a group

1. Open the Amazon EC2 console at https://console.aws.amazon.com/ec2/.

2. On the navigation pane, under **Auto Scaling**, choose **Auto Scaling Groups**.

3. Select your group.

4. On the **Details** tab, choose **Edit**.

5. Do one of the following:

    1. [Classic Load Balancers] For **Load Balancers**, remove the load balancer.

    2. [Target groups] For **Target Groups**, remove the target group.

6. Choose **Save**.

Add a Load Balancer Using the AWS CLI

To attach a Classic Load Balancer
Use the following attach-load-balancers command to attach the specified load balancer to your Auto Scaling group:

```
1 aws autoscaling attach-load-balancers --auto-scaling-group-name my-asg --load-balancer-names my-
    lb
```

To attach a target group
Use the following attach-load-balancer-target-groups command to attach the specified target group to your Auto Scaling group:

```
1 aws autoscaling attach-load-balancer-target-groups --auto-scaling-group-name my-asg --target-
    group-arns my-targetgroup-arn
```

To detach a Classic Load Balancer
Use the following detach-load-balancers command to detach a load balancer from your Auto Scaling group if you no longer need it:

```
1 aws autoscaling detach-load-balancers --auto-scaling-group-name my-asg --load-balancer-names my-
    lb
```

To detach a target group
Use the following detach-load-balancer-target-groups command to detach a target group from your Auto Scaling group if you no longer need it:

```
1 aws autoscaling detach-load-balancer-target-groups --auto-scaling-group-name my-asg --target-
    group-arns my-targetgroup-arn
```

Using ELB Health Checks with Auto Scaling

An Auto Scaling group periodically checks the health status of each instance. It can use EC2 status checks only, or EC2 status checks plus Elastic Load Balancing health checks. If it determines that an instance is unhealthy, it replaces the instance.

If you configure an Auto Scaling group to determine health status using EC2 status checks only, which is the default, It considers the instance unhealthy if it fails the EC2 status checks. However, if you have attached one or more load balancers or target groups to the Auto Scaling group and a load balancer reports that an instance is unhealthy, it does not consider the instance unhealthy and therefore it does not replace it.

If you configure your Auto Scaling group to determine health status using both EC2 status checks and Elastic Load Balancing health checks, it considers the instance unhealthy if it fails either the status checks or the health check. Note that if you attach multiple load balancers to an Auto Scaling group, all of them must report that the instance is healthy in order for it to consider the instance healthy. If one load balancer reports an instance as unhealthy, the Auto Scaling group replaces the instance, even if other load balancers report it as healthy.

For more information, see Health Checks for Auto Scaling Instances.

Topics

- Adding Health Checks Using the Console
- Adding Health Checks Using the AWS CLI

Adding Health Checks Using the Console

Use the following procedure to add an ELB health check with a grace period of 300 seconds to an Auto Scaling group with an attached load balancer.

To add health checks using the console

1. Open the Amazon EC2 console at https://console.aws.amazon.com/ec2/.

2. On the navigation pane, under **Auto Scaling**, choose **Auto Scaling Groups**.

3. Select your group.

4. On the **Details** tab, choose **Edit**.

5. For **Health Check Type**, select ELB.

6. For **Health Check Grace Period**, enter 300.

7. Choose **Save**.

8. On the **Instances** tab, the **Health Status** column displays the results of the newly added health checks.

Adding Health Checks Using the AWS CLI

Use the following update-auto-scaling-group command to create a health check with a grace period of 300 seconds:

```
1 aws autoscaling update-auto-scaling-group --auto-scaling-group-name my-lb-asg --health-check-
    type ELB --health-check-grace-period 300
```

Expanding Your Scaled and Load-Balanced Application to an Additional Availability Zone

You can take advantage of the safety and reliability of geographic redundancy by spanning your Auto Scaling group across multiple Availability Zones within a region and then attaching a load balancer to distribute incoming traffic across those Availability Zones. Incoming traffic is distributed equally across all Availability Zones enabled for your load balancer.

Note
An Auto Scaling group can contain EC2 instances from multiple Availability Zones within the same region. However, an Auto Scaling group can't contain EC2 instances from multiple regions.

When one Availability Zone becomes unhealthy or unavailable, Amazon EC2 Auto Scaling launches new instances in an unaffected Availability Zone. When the unhealthy Availability Zone returns to a healthy state, Amazon EC2 Auto Scaling automatically redistributes the application instances evenly across all of the Availability Zones for your Auto Scaling group. Amazon EC2 Auto Scaling does this by attempting to launch new instances in the Availability Zone with the fewest instances. If the attempt fails, however, Amazon EC2 Auto Scaling attempts to launch in other Availability Zones until it succeeds.

You can expand the availability of your scaled and load-balanced application by adding an Availability Zone to your Auto Scaling group and then enabling that Availability Zone for your load balancer. After you've enabled the new Availability Zone, the load balancer begins to route traffic equally among all the enabled Availability Zones.

Topics
- Add an Availability Zone Using the Console
- Add an Availability Zone Using the AWS CLI

Add an Availability Zone Using the Console

Use the following procedure to expand your Auto Scaling group to an additional subnet (EC2-VPC) or Availability Zone (EC2-Classic).

1. Open the Amazon EC2 console at https://console.aws.amazon.com/ec2/.

2. On the navigation pane, under **Auto Scaling**, choose **Auto Scaling Groups**.

3. Select your group.

4. On the **Details** tab, choose **Edit**.

5. Do one of the following:
   - [EC2-VPC] In **Subnet(s)**, select the subnet corresponding to the Availability Zone.
   - [EC2-Classic] In **Availability Zones(s)**, select the Availability Zone.

6. Choose **Save**.

7. On the navigation pane, choose **Load Balancers**.

8. Select your load balancer.

9. Do one of the following:
   - [Classic Load Balancer in EC2-Classic] On the **Instances** tab, choose **Edit Availability Zones**. On the **Add and Remove Availability Zones** page, select the Availability Zone to add.
   - [Classic Load Balancer in a VPC] On the **Instances** tab, choose **Edit Availability Zones**. On the **Add and Remove Subnets** page, for **Available subnets**, choose the add icon (+) for the subnet to add. The subnet is moved under **Selected subnets**.

- [Application Load Balancer] On the **Description** tab, for **Availability Zones**, choose **Edit**. Choose the add icon (+) for one of the subnets for the Availability Zone to add. The subnet is moved under **Selected subnets**.

10. Choose **Save**.

Add an Availability Zone Using the AWS CLI

The commands that you'll use depend on whether your load balancer is a Classic Load Balancer in a VPC, a Classic Load Balancer in EC2-Classic, or an Application Load Balancer.

For an Auto Scaling group with a Classic Load Balancer in a VPC

1. Add a subnet to the Auto Scaling group using the following update-auto-scaling-group command:

```
1 aws autoscaling update-auto-scaling-group --auto-scaling-group-name my-asg --vpc-zone-
    identifier subnet-41767929 subnet-cb663da2 --min-size 2
```

2. Verify that the instances in the new subnet are ready to accept traffic from the load balancer using the following describe-auto-scaling-groups command:

```
1 aws autoscaling describe-auto-scaling-groups --auto-scaling-group-name my-asg
```

3. Enable the new subnet for your Classic Load Balancer using the following attach-load-balancer-to-subnets command:

```
1 aws elb attach-load-balancer-to-subnets --load-balancer-name my-lb --subnets subnet
    -41767929
```

For an Auto Scaling group with a Classic Load Balancer in EC2-Classic

1. Add an Availability Zone to the Auto Scaling group using the following update-auto-scaling-group command:

```
1 aws autoscaling update-auto-scaling-group --auto-scaling-group-name my-asg --availability-
    zones us-west-2a us-west-2b us-west-2c --min-size 3
```

2. Verify that the instances in the new Availability Zone are ready to accept traffic from the load balancer using the following describe-auto-scaling-groups command:

```
1 aws autoscaling describe-auto-scaling-groups --auto-scaling-group-name my-asg
```

3. Enable the new Availability Zone for your Classic Load Balancer using the following enable-availability-zones-for-load-balancer command:

```
1 aws elb enable-availability-zones-for-load-balancer --load-balancer-name my-lb --
    availability-zones us-west-2c
```

For an Auto Scaling group with an Application Load Balancer

1. Add a subnet to the Auto Scaling group using the following update-auto-scaling-group command:

```
1 aws autoscaling update-auto-scaling-group --auto-scaling-group-name my-asg --vpc-zone-
    identifier subnet-41767929 subnet-cb663da2 --min-size 2
```

2. Verify that the instances in the new subnet are ready to accept traffic from the load balancer using the following describe-auto-scaling-groups command:

```
1 aws autoscaling describe-auto-scaling-groups --auto-scaling-group-name my-asg
```

3. Enable the new subnet for your Application Load Balancer using the following set-subnets command:

```
1 aws elbv2 set-subnets --load-balancer-arn my-lb-arn --subnets subnet-41767929 subnet-
    cb663da2
```

Launching Spot Instances in Your Auto Scaling Group

Spot Instances are a cost-effective choice compared to On-Demand instances, if you can be flexible about when your applications run and if your applications can be interrupted. You can configure your Auto Scaling group to launch Spot Instances instead of On-Demand instances.

Before launching Spot Instances using Amazon EC2 Auto Scaling, we recommend that you become familiar with launching and managing Spot Instances using Amazon EC2. For more information, see Spot Instances in the *Amazon EC2 User Guide for Linux Instances*.

Here's how Spot Instances work with Amazon EC2 Auto Scaling:

- **Setting your maximum price.** You can set the maximum price you are willing to pay in the launch configuration or launch template. You can't launch both On-Demand instances and Spot Instances.
- **Changing your maximum price.** You must create a launch configuration or launch template with the new price. With a new launch configuration, you must associate it with your Auto Scaling group. With a launch template, you can configure the Auto Scaling group to use the default template or the latest version of the template, so it will automatically be associated with the Auto Scaling group. Note that the existing instances continue to run as long as the maximum price specified in the launch configuration or launch template used for those instances is higher than the current Spot market price.
- **Spot market price and your maximum price.** If the market price for Spot Instances rises above your maximum price for a running instance in your Auto Scaling group, Amazon EC2 terminates your instance. If your maximum price exactly matches the Spot market price, whether your request is fulfilled depends on several factors—such as available Spot Instance capacity.
- **Maintaining your Spot Instances.** When your Spot Instance is terminated, the Auto Scaling group attempts to launch a replacement instance to maintain the desired capacity for the group. If your maximum price is higher than the Spot market price, then it launches a Spot Instance. Otherwise, it keeps trying.
- **Balancing across Availability Zones.** If you specify multiple Availability Zones, Auto Scaling distributes the Spot requests across these Availability Zones. If your maximum price is too low in one Availability Zone for any requests to be fulfilled, Amazon EC2 Auto Scaling checks whether requests were fulfilled in the other Availability Zones. If so, Amazon EC2 Auto Scaling cancels the requests that failed and redistributes them across the Availability Zones that have requests fulfilled. If the price in an Availability Zone with no fulfilled requests drops enough that future requests succeed, Auto Scaling rebalances across all the Availability Zones. For more information, see Rebalancing Activities.
- **Spot Instance termination.** Amazon EC2 Auto Scaling can terminate or replace Spot Instances just as it can terminate or replace On-Demand instances. For more information, see Controlling Which Auto Scaling Instances Terminate During Scale In.

Merging Your Auto Scaling Groups into a Single Multi-Zone Group

To merge separate single-zone Auto Scaling groups into a single Auto Scaling group spanning multiple Availability Zones, rezone one of the single-zone groups into a multi-zone group, and then delete the other groups. This process works for groups with or without a load balancer, as long as the new multi-zone group is in one of the same Availability Zones as the original single-zone groups.

The following examples assume that you have two identical groups in two different Availability Zones, us-west-2a and us-west-2c. These two groups share the following specifications:

- Minimum size = 2
- Maximum size = 5
- Desired capacity = 3

Merge Zones Using the AWS CLI

Use the following procedure to merge my-group-a and my-group-c into a single group that covers both us-west-2a and us-west-2c.

To merge separate single-zone groups into a single multi-zone group

1. Use the following update-auto-scaling-group command to add the us-west-2c Availability Zone to the supported Availability Zones for my-group-a and increase the maximum size of this group to allow for the instances from both single-zone groups:

```
1 aws autoscaling update-auto-scaling-group --auto-scaling-group-name my-group-a --
    availability-zones "us-west-2a" "us-west-2c" --max-size 10 --min-size 4
```

2. Use the following set-desired-capacity command to increase the size of my-group-a:

```
1 aws autoscaling set-desired-capacity --auto-scaling-group-name my-group-a --desired-
    capacity 6
```

3. (Optional) Use the following describe-auto-scaling-groups command to verify that my-group-a is at its new size:

```
1 aws autoscaling describe-auto-scaling-groups --auto-scaling-group-name my-group-a
```

4. Use the following update-auto-scaling-group command to remove the instances from my-group-c:

```
1 aws autoscaling update-auto-scaling-group --auto-scaling-group-name my-group-c --min-size 0
    --max-size 0
```

5. (Optional) Use the following describe-auto-scaling-groups command to verify that no instances remain in my-group-c:

```
1 aws autoscaling describe-auto-scaling-groups --auto-scaling-group-name my-group-c
```

The following is example output:

```
1 {
2     "AutoScalingGroups": [
3         {
4             "AutoScalingGroupARN": "arn",
5             "HealthCheckGracePeriod": 300,
6             "SuspendedProcesses": [],
7             "DesiredCapacity": 0,
8             "Tags": [],
```

```
9      "EnabledMetrics": [],
10     "LoadBalancerNames": [],
11     "AutoScalingGroupName": "my-group-c",
12     "DefaultCooldown": 300,
13     "MinSize": 0,
14     "Instances": [],
15     "MaxSize": 0,
16     "VPCZoneIdentifier": "null",
17     "TerminationPolicies": [
18         "Default"
19     ],
20     "LaunchConfigurationName": "my-lc",
21     "CreatedTime": "2015-02-26T18:24:14.449Z",
22     "AvailabilityZones": [
23         "us-west-2c"
24     ],
25     "HealthCheckType": "EC2"
26   }
27  ]
28 }
```

6. Use the delete-auto-scaling-group command to delete my-group-c:

```
1 aws autoscaling delete-auto-scaling-group --auto-scaling-group-name my-group-c
```

Deleting Your Auto Scaling Infrastructure

To completely delete your scaling infrastructure, complete the following tasks.

Topics

- Delete Your Auto Scaling Group
- (Optional) Delete the Launch Configuration
- (Optional) Delete the Load Balancer
- (Optional) Delete CloudWatch Alarms

Delete Your Auto Scaling Group

When you delete an Auto Scaling group, its desired, minimum, and maximum values are set to 0. As a result, the Auto Scaling instances are terminated. Alternatively, you can terminate or detach the instances before you delete the Auto Scaling group.

To delete your Auto Scaling group using the console

1. Open the Amazon EC2 console at https://console.aws.amazon.com/ec2/.

2. On the navigation pane, under **Auto Scaling**, choose **Auto Scaling Groups**.

3. On the Auto Scaling groups page, select your Auto Scaling group. and choose **Actions, Delete**.

4. When prompted for confirmation, choose **Yes, Delete**.

To delete your Auto Scaling group using the AWS CLI
Use the following delete-auto-scaling-group command to delete the Auto Scaling group:

```
1 aws autoscaling delete-auto-scaling-group --auto-scaling-group-name my-asg
```

(Optional) Delete the Launch Configuration

Note that you can skip this step if you want to keep the launch configuration for future use.

To delete the launch configuration using the console

1. On the navigation pane, under **Auto Scaling**, choose **Launch Configurations**.

2. On the **Launch Configurations** page, select your launch configuration and choose **Actions, Delete launch configuration**.

3. When prompted for confirmation, choose **Yes, Delete**.

To delete the launch configuration using the AWS CLI
Use the following delete-launch-configuration command:

```
1 aws autoscaling delete-launch-configuration --launch-configuration-name my-lc
```

(Optional) Delete the Load Balancer

Note that you can skip this step if your Auto Scaling group is not registered with an Elastic Load Balancing load balancer or you want to keep the load balancer for future use.

To delete your load balancer

1. On the navigation pane, under **LOAD BALANCING**, choose **Load Balancers**.

2. Select the load balancer and choose **Actions, Delete**.

3. When prompted for confirmation, choose **Yes, Delete**.

To delete the load balancer associated with the Auto Scaling group using the AWS CLI

For Application Load Balancers and Network Load Balancers, use the following delete-load-balancer command:

```
1 aws elbv2 delete-load-balancer --load-balancer-arn my-load-balancer-arn
```

For Classic Load Balancers, use the following delete-load-balancer command:

```
1 aws elb delete-load-balancer --load-balancer-name my-load-balancer
```

(Optional) Delete CloudWatch Alarms

Note that you can skip this step if your Auto Scaling group is not associated with any CloudWatch alarms or you want to keep the alarms for future use.

To delete the CloudWatch alarms using the console

1. Open the CloudWatch console at https://console.aws.amazon.com/cloudwatch/.

2. On the navigation pane, choose **Alarms**.

3. Select the alarms and choose **Delete**.

4. When prompted for confirmation, choose **Yes, Delete**.

To delete the CloudWatch alarms using the AWS CLI

Use the delete-alarms command. For example, use the following command to delete the `AddCapacity` and `RemoveCapacity` alarms:

```
1 aws cloudwatch delete-alarms --alarm-name AddCapacity RemoveCapacity
```

Scaling the Size of Your Auto Scaling Group

Scaling is the ability to increase or decrease the compute capacity of your application. Scaling starts with an event, or scaling action, which instructs an Auto Scaling group to either launch or terminate EC2 instances.

Amazon EC2 Auto Scaling provides a number of ways to adjust scaling to best meet the needs of your applications. As a result, it's important that you have a good understanding of your application. Keep the following considerations in mind:

- What role do you want Amazon EC2 Auto Scaling to play in your application's architecture? It's common to think about automatic scaling as a way to increase and decrease capacity, but it's also useful for maintaining a steady number of servers.
- What cost constraints are important to you? Because Amazon EC2 Auto Scaling uses EC2 instances, you only pay for the resources that you use. Knowing your cost constraints helps you decide when to scale your applications, and by how much.
- What metrics are important to your application? CloudWatch supports a number of different metrics that you can use with your Auto Scaling group. We recommend reviewing them to see which of these metrics are the most relevant to your application.

Topics

- Scaling Options
- Multiple Scaling Policies
- Maintaining the Size of Your Auto Scaling Group
- Manual Scaling
- Scheduled Scaling
- Dynamic Scaling
- Scaling Cooldowns
- Auto Scaling Instance Termination
- Lifecycle Hooks
- Temporarily Removing Instances
- Suspending and Resuming Scaling Processes

Scaling Options

Amazon EC2 Auto Scaling provides several ways for you to scale your Auto Scaling group.

Maintain current instance levels at all times
You can configure your Auto Scaling group to maintain a minimum or specified number of running instances at all times. To maintain the current instance levels, Amazon EC2 Auto Scaling performs a periodic health check on running instances within an Auto Scaling group. When Amazon EC2 Auto Scaling finds an unhealthy instance, it terminates that instance and launches a new one. For information about configuring your Auto Scaling group to maintain the current instance levels, see Maintaining the Number of Instances in Your Auto Scaling Group.

Manual scaling
Manual scaling is the most basic way to scale your resources. Specify only the change in the maximum, minimum, or desired capacity of your Auto Scaling group. Amazon EC2 Auto Scaling manages the process of creating or terminating instances to maintain the updated capacity. For more information, see Manual Scaling.

Scale based on a schedule
Sometimes you know exactly when you will need to increase or decrease the number of instances in your group, simply because that need arises on a predictable schedule. Scaling by schedule means that scaling actions are performed automatically as a function of time and date. For more information, see Scheduled Scaling for Amazon EC2 Auto Scaling.

Scale based on demand
A more advanced way to scale your resources, scaling by policy, lets you define parameters that control the

scaling process. For example, you can create a policy that calls for enlarging your fleet of EC2 instances whenever the average CPU utilization rate stays above ninety percent for fifteen minutes. This is useful when you can define how you want to scale in response to changing conditions, but you don't know when those conditions will change. You can set up Amazon EC2 Auto Scaling to respond for you.

You should have two policies, one for scaling in (terminating instances) and one for scaling out (launching instances), for each event to monitor. For example, if you want to scale out when the network bandwidth reaches a certain level, create a policy specifying that Amazon EC2 Auto Scaling should start a certain number of instances to help with your traffic. But you may also want an accompanying policy to scale in by a certain number when the network bandwidth level goes back down. For more information, see Dynamic Scaling for Amazon EC2 Auto Scaling.

Multiple Scaling Policies

An Auto Scaling group can have more than one scaling policy attached to it any given time. In fact, we recommend that each Auto Scaling group has at least two policies: one to scale your architecture out and another to scale your architecture in. You can also combine scaling policies to maximize the performance of an Auto Scaling group.

To illustrate how multiple policies work together, consider an application that uses an Auto Scaling group and an Amazon SQS queue to send requests to the EC2 instances in that group. To help ensure that the application performs at optimum levels, there are two policies that control when the Auto Scaling group should scale out. One policy uses the Amazon CloudWatch metric, `CPUUtilization`, to detect when an instance is at 90% of capacity. The other uses the `NumberOfMessagesVisible` to detect when the SQS queue is becoming overwhelmed with messages.

Note
In a production environment, both of these policies would have complementary policies that control when Amazon EC2 Auto Scaling should scale in the number of EC2 instances.

When you have more than one policy attached to an Auto Scaling group, there's a chance that both policies could instruct it to scale out (or in) at the same time. In our previous example, it's possible that both an EC2 instance could trigger the CloudWatch alarm for the `CPUUtilization` metric, and the SQS queue trigger the alarm for the `NumberOfMessagesVisible` metric.

When these situations occur, Amazon EC2 Auto Scaling chooses the policy that has the greatest impact on the Auto Scaling group. For example, suppose that the policy for CPU utilization launches one instance, while the policy for the SQS queue launches two instances. If the scale-out criteria for both policies are met at the same time, Amazon EC2 Auto Scaling gives precedence to the SQS queue policy, because it has the greatest impact on the Auto Scaling group. This results in the Auto Scaling group launching two instances. This precedence applies even when the policies use different criteria for scaling out. For instance, if one policy launches three instances, and another increases capacity by 25 percent, Amazon EC2 Auto Scaling give precedence to whichever policy has the greatest impact on the group at that time.

Maintaining the Number of Instances in Your Auto Scaling Group

After you have created your launch configuration and Auto Scaling group, the Auto Scaling group starts by launching the minimum number of EC2 instances (or the desired capacity, if specified). If there are no other scaling conditions attached to the Auto Scaling group, the Auto Scaling group maintains this number of running instances at all times.

To maintain the same number of instances, Amazon EC2 Auto Scaling performs a periodic health check on running instances within an Auto Scaling group. When it finds that an instance is unhealthy, it terminates that instance and launches a new one.

All instances in your Auto Scaling group start in the healthy state. Instances are assumed to be healthy unless Amazon EC2 Auto Scaling receives notification that they are unhealthy. This notification can come from one or more of the following sources: Amazon EC2, Elastic Load Balancing, or your customized health check.

Determining Instance Health

By default, the Auto Scaling group determines the health state of each instance by periodically checking the results of EC2 instance status checks. If the instance status is any state other than `running` or if the system status is `impaired`, Amazon EC2 Auto Scaling considers the instance to be unhealthy and launches a replacement. For more information about EC2 instance status checks, see Monitoring the Status of Your Instances in the *Amazon EC2 User Guide for Linux Instances*.

If you have associated your Auto Scaling group with a load balancer or a target group and have chosen to use the ELB health checks, Amazon EC2 Auto Scaling determines the health status of the instances by checking both the instance status checks and the ELB health checks. Amazon EC2 Auto Scaling marks an instance as unhealthy if the instance is in a state other than `running`, the system status is `impaired`, or Elastic Load Balancing reports that the instance failed the health checks.

You can customize the health check conducted by your Auto Scaling group by specifying additional checks. Or, if you have your own health check system, you can send the instance's health information directly from your system to Amazon EC2 Auto Scaling.

Replacing Unhealthy Instances

After an instance has been marked unhealthy because of an Amazon EC2 or Elastic Load Balancing health check, it is almost immediately scheduled for replacement. It never automatically recovers its health. You can intervene manually by calling the SetInstanceHealth action (or the `as-set-instance-health` command) to set the instance's health status back to healthy. If the instance is already terminating, you get an error. Because the interval between marking an instance unhealthy and its actual termination is so small, attempting to set an instance's health status back to healthy with the `SetInstanceHealth` action (or, `as-set-instance-health` command) is probably useful only for a suspended group. For more information, see Suspending and Resuming Scaling Processes.

Amazon EC2 Auto Scaling creates a new scaling activity for terminating the unhealthy instance and then terminates it. Later, another scaling activity launches a new instance to replace the terminated instance.

When your instance is terminated, any associated Elastic IP addresses are disassociated and are not automatically associated with the new instance. You must associate these Elastic IP addresses with the new instance manually. Similarly, when your instance is terminated, its attached EBS volumes are detached. You must attach these EBS volumes to the new instance manually.

Manual Scaling

At any time, you can change the size of an existing Auto Scaling group. Update the desired capacity of the Auto Scaling group, or update the instances that are attached to the Auto Scaling group.

Topics

- Change the Size of Your Auto Scaling Group Using the Console
- Change the Size of Your Auto Scaling Group Using the AWS CLI
- Attach EC2 Instances to Your Auto Scaling Group
- Detach EC2 Instances from Your Auto Scaling Group

Change the Size of Your Auto Scaling Group Using the Console

When you change the size of your Auto Scaling group, Amazon EC2 Auto Scaling manages the process of launching or terminating instances to maintain the new group size.

The following example assumes that you've created an Auto Scaling group with a minimum size of 1 and a maximum size of 5. Therefore, the group currently has one running instance.

To change the size of your Auto Scaling group

1. Open the Amazon EC2 console at https://console.aws.amazon.com/ec2/.

2. On the navigation pane, under **Auto Scaling**, choose **Auto Scaling Groups**.

3. Select your Auto Scaling group.

4. On the **Details** tab, choose **Edit**.

5. For **Desired**, increase the desired capacity by one. For example, if the current value is 1, type 2.

   The desired capacity must be less than or equal to the maximum size of the group. If your new value for **Desired** is greater than **Max**, you must update **Max** .

   When you are finished, choose **Save**.

Now, verify that your Auto Scaling group has launched one additional instance.

To verify that the size of your Auto Scaling group has changed

1. On the **Activity History** tab, the **Status** column shows the current status of your instance. You can use the refresh button until you see the status of your instance change to **Successful**, indicating that your Auto Scaling group has successfully launched a new instance.

2. On the **Instances** tab, the **Lifecycle** column shows the state of your instances. It takes a short time for an instance to launch. After the instance starts, its state changes to InService. You can see that your Auto Scaling group has launched 1 new instance, and it is in the InService state.

Change the Size of Your Auto Scaling Group Using the AWS CLI

When you change the size of your Auto Scaling group, Amazon EC2 Auto Scaling manages the process of launching or terminating instances to maintain the new group size.

The following example assumes that you've created an Auto Scaling group with a minimum size of 1 and a maximum size of 5. Therefore, the group currently has one running instance.

Use the set-desired-capacity command to change the size of your Auto Scaling group, as shown in the following example:

```
1 aws autoscaling set-desired-capacity --auto-scaling-group-name my-asg --desired-capacity 2
```

By default, the command does not wait for the cooldown period specified for the group to complete. You can override the default behavior and wait for the cooldown period to complete by specifying the `-honor-cooldown` option as shown in the following example. For more information, see Scaling Cooldowns for Amazon EC2 Auto Scaling.

```
1 aws autoscaling set-desired-capacity --auto-scaling-group-name my-asg --desired-capacity 2 --
    honor-cooldown
```

Use the describe-auto-scaling-groups command to confirm that the size of your Auto Scaling group has changed, as in the following example:

```
1 aws autoscaling describe-auto-scaling-groups --auto-scaling-group-name my-asg
```

The following is example output, with details about the group and instances launched.

```
1  {
2      "AutoScalingGroups": [
3          {
4              "AutoScalingGroupARN": "arn",
5              "HealthCheckGracePeriod": 300,
6              "SuspendedProcesses": [],
7              "DesiredCapacity": 2,
8              "Tags": [],
9              "EnabledMetrics": [],
10             "LoadBalancerNames": [],
11             "AutoScalingGroupName": "my-asg",
12             "DefaultCooldown": 300,
13             "MinSize": 1,
14             "Instances": [
15                 {
16                     "InstanceId": "i-33388a3f",
17                     "AvailabilityZone": "us-west-2a",
18                     "HealthStatus": "Healthy",
19                     "LifecycleState": "InService",
20                     "LaunchConfigurationName": "my-lc"
21                 }
22             ],
23             "MaxSize": 5,
24             "VPCZoneIdentifier": "subnet-e4f33493",
25             "TerminationPolicies": [
26                 "Default"
27             ],
28             "LaunchConfigurationName": "my-lc",
29             "CreatedTime": "2014-12-12T23:30:42.611Z",
30             "AvailabilityZones": [
31                 "us-west-2a"
32             ],
33             "HealthCheckType": "EC2"
34         }
35     ]
36 }
```

Notice that `DesiredCapacity` shows the new value. Your Auto Scaling group has launched an additional instance.

Attach EC2 Instances to Your Auto Scaling Group

Amazon EC2 Auto Scaling provides you with an option to enable automatic scaling for one or more EC2 instances by attaching them to your existing Auto Scaling group. After the instances are attached, they become a part of the Auto Scaling group.

The instance that you want to attach must meet the following criteria:

- The instance is in the **running** state.
- The AMI used to launch the instance must still exist.
- The instance is not a member of another Auto Scaling group.
- The instance is in the same Availability Zone as the Auto Scaling group.
- If the Auto Scaling group has an attached load balancer, the instance and the load balancer must both be in EC2-Classic or the same VPC. If the Auto Scaling group has an attached target group, the instance and the load balancer must both be in the same VPC.

When you attach instances, the desired capacity of the group increases by the number of instances being attached. If the number of instances being attached plus the desired capacity exceeds the maximum size of the group, the request fails.

If you attach an instance to an Auto Scaling group that has an attached load balancer, the instance is registered with the load balancer. If you attach an instance to an Auto Scaling group that has an attached target group, the instance is registered with the target group.

Topics

- Attaching an Instance Using the AWS Management Console
- Attaching an Instance Using the AWS CLI

The examples use an Auto Scaling group with the following configuration:

- Auto Scaling group name = **my-asg**
- Minimum size = **1**
- Maximum size = **5**
- Desired capacity = **2**
- Availability Zone = **us-west-2a**

Attaching an Instance Using the AWS Management Console

You can attach an existing instance to an existing Auto Scaling group, or to a new Auto Scaling group as you create it.

To attach an instance to a new Auto Scaling group using the console

1. Open the Amazon EC2 console at https://console.aws.amazon.com/ec2/.

2. On the navigation pane, choose **Instances**.

3. Select the instance.

4. Choose **Actions, Instance Settings, Attach to Auto Scaling Group**.

5. On the **Attach to Auto Scaling Group** page, select **a new Auto Scaling group**, type a name for the group, and then choose **Attach**.

   The new Auto Scaling group is created using a new launch configuration with the same name that you specified for the Auto Scaling group. The launch configuration gets its settings (for example, security group and IAM role) from the instance that you attached. The Auto Scaling group gets settings (for example, Availability Zone and subnet) from the instance that you attached, and has a desired capacity and maximum size of **1**.

6. (Optional) To edit the settings for the Auto Scaling group, on the navigation pane, under **Auto Scaling**, choose **Auto Scaling Groups**. Select the new Auto Scaling group, choose **Edit**, change the settings as needed, and then choose **Save**.

To attach an instance to an existing Auto Scaling group using the console

1. Open the Amazon EC2 console at https://console.aws.amazon.com/ec2/.

2. (Optional) On the navigation pane, under **Auto Scaling**, choose **Auto Scaling Groups**. Select the Auto Scaling group and verify that the maximum size of the Auto Scaling group is large enough that you can add another instance. Otherwise, choose **Edit**, increase the maximum size, and then choose **Save**.

3. On the navigation pane, choose **Instances**.

4. Select the instance.

5. Choose **Actions, Instance Settings, Attach to Auto Scaling Group**.

6. On the **Attach to Auto Scaling Group** page, select **an existing Auto Scaling group**, select the instance, and then choose **Attach**.

7. If the instance doesn't meet the criteria (for example, if it's not in the same Availability Zone as the Auto Scaling group), you get an error message with the details. Choose **Close** and try again with an instance that meets the criteria.

Attaching an Instance Using the AWS CLI

To attach an instance to an Auto Scaling group using the AWS CLI

1. Describe a specific Auto Scaling group using the following describe-auto-scaling-groups command:

```
1 aws autoscaling describe-auto-scaling-groups --auto-scaling-group-names my-asg
```

The following example response shows that the desired capacity is 2 and the group has 2 running instances:

```
1  {
2      "AutoScalingGroups": [
3          {
4              "AutoScalingGroupARN": "arn",
5              "HealthCheckGracePeriod": 300,
6              "SuspendedProcesses": [],
7              "DesiredCapacity": 2,
8              "Tags": [],
9              "EnabledMetrics": [],
10             "LoadBalancerNames": [],
11             "AutoScalingGroupName": "my-asg",
12             "DefaultCooldown": 300,
13             "MinSize": 1,
14             "Instances": [
15                 {
16                     "InstanceId": "i-a5e87793",
17                     "AvailabilityZone": "us-west-2a",
18                     "HealthStatus": "Healthy",
19                     "LifecycleState": "InService",
20                     "LaunchConfigurationName": "my-lc"
21                 },
22                 {
23                     "InstanceId": "i-a4e87792",
24                     "AvailabilityZone": "us-west-2a",
```

```
25              "HealthStatus": "Healthy",
26              "LifecycleState": "InService",
27              "LaunchConfigurationName": "my-lc"
28          }
29      ],
30      "MaxSize": 5,
31      "VPCZoneIdentifier": "subnet-e4f33493",
32      "TerminationPolicies": [
33          "Default"
34      ],
35      "LaunchConfigurationName": "my-lc",
36      "CreatedTime": "2014-12-12T23:30:42.611Z",
37      "AvailabilityZones": [
38          "us-west-2a"
39      ],
40      "HealthCheckType": "EC2"
41      }
42  ]
43 }
```

2. Attach an instance to the Auto Scaling group using the following attach-instances command:

```
1 aws autoscaling attach-instances --instance-ids i-a8e09d9c --auto-scaling-group-name my-asg
```

3. To verify that the instance is attached, use the following describe-auto-scaling-groups command:

```
1 aws autoscaling describe-auto-scaling-groups --auto-scaling-group-names my-asg
```

The following example response shows that the desired capacity has increased by 1 to 3, and that there is a new instance, i-a8e09d9c:

```
1 {
2      "AutoScalingGroups": [
3          {
4              "AutoScalingGroupARN": "arn",
5              "HealthCheckGracePeriod": 300,
6              "SuspendedProcesses": [],
7              "DesiredCapacity": 3,
8              "Tags": [],
9              "EnabledMetrics": [],
10             "LoadBalancerNames": [],
11             "AutoScalingGroupName": "my-asg",
12             "DefaultCooldown": 300,
13             "MinSize": 1,
14             "Instances": [
15                 {
16                     "InstanceId": "i-a8e09d9c",
17                     "AvailabilityZone": "us-west-2a",
18                     "HealthStatus": "Healthy",
19                     "LifecycleState": "InService",
20                     "LaunchConfigurationName": "my-lc"
21                 },
22                 {
23                     "InstanceId": "i-a5e87793",
24                     "AvailabilityZone": "us-west-2a",
25                     "HealthStatus": "Healthy",
```

```
26          "LifecycleState": "InService",
27          "LaunchConfigurationName": "my-lc"
28      },
29      {
30          "InstanceId": "i-a4e87792",
31          "AvailabilityZone": "us-west-2a",
32          "HealthStatus": "Healthy",
33          "LifecycleState": "InService",
34          "LaunchConfigurationName": "my-lc"
35      }
36  ],
37  "MaxSize": 5,
38  "VPCZoneIdentifier": "subnet-e4f33493",
39  "TerminationPolicies": [
40      "Default"
41  ],
42  "LaunchConfigurationName": "my-lc",
43  "CreatedTime": "2014-12-12T23:30:42.611Z",
44  "AvailabilityZones": [
45      "us-west-2a"
46  ],
47  "HealthCheckType": "EC2"
48      }
49  ]
50 }
```

Detach EC2 Instances from Your Auto Scaling Group

You can remove an instance from an Auto Scaling group. After the instances are detached, you can manage them independently from the rest of the Auto Scaling group. By detaching an instance, you can:

- Move an instance out of one Auto Scaling group and attach it to a different one. For more information, see Attach EC2 Instances to Your Auto Scaling Group.
- Test an Auto Scaling group by creating it using existing instances running your application, and then detach these instances from the Auto Scaling group when your tests are complete.

When you detach instances, you have the option of decrementing the desired capacity for the Auto Scaling group by the number of instances being detached. If you choose not to decrement the capacity, Amazon EC2 Auto Scaling launches new instances to replace the ones that you detached. If you decrement the capacity but detach multiple instances from the same Availability Zone, Amazon EC2 Auto Scaling can rebalance the Availability Zones unless you suspend the `AZRebalance` process. For more information, see Scaling Processes.

If the number of instances that you are detaching would drop the size of the Auto Scaling group below its minimum capacity, you must decrement the minimum capacity for the Auto Scaling group before you can detach the instances.

If you detach an instance from an Auto Scaling group that has an attached load balancer, the instance is deregistered from the load balancer. If you detach an instance from an Auto Scaling group that has an attached target group, the instance is deregistered from the target group. If connection draining is enabled for your load balancer, Amazon EC2 Auto Scaling waits for in-flight requests to complete.

Topics

- Detaching Instances Using the AWS Management Console
- Detaching Instances Using the AWS CLI

The examples use an Auto Scaling group with the following configuration:

- Auto Scaling group name = `my-asg`
- Minimum size = 1
- Maximum size = 5
- Desired capacity = 4
- Availability Zone = `us-west-2a`

Detaching Instances Using the AWS Management Console

Use the following procedure to detach an instance from your Auto Scaling group.

To detach an instance from an existing Auto Scaling group using the console

1. Open the Amazon EC2 console at https://console.aws.amazon.com/ec2/.
2. On the navigation pane, under **Auto Scaling**, choose **Auto Scaling Groups**.
3. Select your Auto Scaling group.
4. On the **Instances** tab, select the instance and choose **Actions**, **Detach**.
5. On the **Detach Instance** page, select the check box to launch a replacement instance, or leave it unchecked to decrement the desired capacity. Choose **Detach Instance**.

Detaching Instances Using the AWS CLI

Use the following procedure to detach an instance from your Auto Scaling group.

To detach an instance from an existing Auto Scaling group using the AWS CLI

1. List the current instances using the following describe-auto-scaling-instances command:

```
1 aws autoscaling describe-auto-scaling-instances
```

The following example response shows that the group has 4 running instances:

```
1 {
2     "AutoScalingInstances": [
3         {
4             "AvailabilityZone": "us-west-2a",
5             "InstanceId": "i-2a2d8978",
6             "AutoScalingGroupName": "my-asg",
7             "HealthStatus": "HEALTHY",
8             "LifecycleState": "InService",
9             "LaunchConfigurationName": "my-lc"
10        },
11        {
12            "AvailabilityZone": "us-west-2a",
13            "InstanceId": "i-5f2e8a0d",
14            "AutoScalingGroupName": "my-asg",
15            "HealthStatus": "HEALTHY",
16            "LifecycleState": "InService",
17            "LaunchConfigurationName": "my-lc"
18        }
19        {
20            "AvailabilityZone": "us-west-2a",
21            "InstanceId": "i-a52387f7",
22            "AutoScalingGroupName": "my-asg",
23            "HealthStatus": "HEALTHY",
24            "LifecycleState": "InService",
25            "LaunchConfigurationName": "my-lc"
26        }
27        {
28            "AvailabilityZone": "us-west-2a",
29            "InstanceId": "i-f42d89a6",
30            "AutoScalingGroupName": "my-asg",
31            "HealthStatus": "HEALTHY",
32            "LifecycleState": "InService",
33            "LaunchConfigurationName": "my-lc"
34        }
35    ]
36 }
```

2. Detach an instance and decrement the desired capacity using the following detach-instances command:

```
1 aws autoscaling detach-instances --instance-ids i-2a2d8978 --auto-scaling-group-name my-asg
    --should-decrement-desired-capacity
```

3. Verify that the instance is detached using the following describe-auto-scaling-instances command:

```
1 aws autoscaling describe-auto-scaling-instances
```

The following example response shows that there are now 3 running instances:

```
1 {
2     "AutoScalingInstances": [
3         {
```

```
 4          "AvailabilityZone": "us-west-2a",
 5          "InstanceId": "i-5f2e8a0d",
 6          "AutoScalingGroupName": "my-asg",
 7          "HealthStatus": "HEALTHY",
 8          "LifecycleState": "InService",
 9          "LaunchConfigurationName": "my-lc"
10      }
11      {
12          "AvailabilityZone": "us-west-2a",
13          "InstanceId": "i-a52387f7",
14          "AutoScalingGroupName": "my-asg",
15          "HealthStatus": "HEALTHY",
16          "LifecycleState": "InService",
17          "LaunchConfigurationName": "my-lc"
18      }
19      {
20          "AvailabilityZone": "us-west-2a",
21          "InstanceId": "i-f42d89a6",
22          "AutoScalingGroupName": "my-asg",
23          "HealthStatus": "HEALTHY",
24          "LifecycleState": "InService",
25          "LaunchConfigurationName": "my-lc"
26      }
27  ]
28 }
```

Scheduled Scaling for Amazon EC2 Auto Scaling

Scaling based on a schedule allows you to scale your application in response to predictable load changes. For example, every week the traffic to your web application starts to increase on Wednesday, remains high on Thursday, and starts to decrease on Friday. You can plan your scaling activities based on the predictable traffic patterns of your web application.

To configure your Auto Scaling group to scale based on a schedule, you create a scheduled action, which tells Amazon EC2 Auto Scaling to perform a scaling action at specified times. To create a scheduled scaling action, you specify the start time when you want the scaling action to take effect, and the new minimum, maximum, and desired sizes for the scaling action. At the specified time, Amazon EC2 Auto Scaling updates the group with the values for minimum, maximum, and desired size specified by the scaling action.

You can create scheduled actions for scaling one time only or for scaling on a recurring schedule.

You can also use scheduled scaling with Application Auto Scaling. For more information, see Scheduled Scaling in the *Application Auto Scaling User Guide*.

Topics

- Considerations for Scheduled Actions
- Create a Scheduled Action Using the Console
- Update a Scheduled Action
- Create or Update a Scheduled Action Using the AWS CLI
- Delete a Scheduled Action

Considerations for Scheduled Actions

When you create a scheduled action, keep the following in mind.

- The order of execution for scheduled actions is guaranteed within the same group, but not for scheduled actions across groups.
- A scheduled action generally executes within seconds. However, the action may be delayed for up to two minutes from the scheduled start time. Because actions within an Auto Scaling group are executed in the order they are specified, scheduled actions with scheduled start times close to each other can take longer to execute.
- You can create a maximum of 125 scheduled actions per Auto Scaling group.
- A scheduled action must have a unique time value. If you attempt to schedule an activity at a time when another scaling activity is already scheduled, the call is rejected with an error message noting the conflict.
- Cooldown periods are not supported.

Create a Scheduled Action Using the Console

Complete the following procedure to create a scheduled action to scale your Auto Scaling group.

To create a scheduled action

1. Open the Amazon EC2 console at https://console.aws.amazon.com/ec2/.

2. On the navigation pane, under **Auto Scaling**, choose **Auto Scaling Groups**.

3. Select your Auto Scaling group.

4. On the **Scheduled Actions** tab, choose **Create Scheduled Action**.

5. On the **Create Scheduled Action** page, do the following:

    - Specify the size of the group using at least one of **Min**, **Max**, and **Desired Capacity**.

- Choose an option for **Recurrence**. If you choose **Once**, the action is performed at the specified time. If you select **Cron**, type a Cron expression that specifies when to perform the action, in UTC. If you select an option that begins with **Every**, the Cron expression is created for you.
- If you chose **Once** for **Recurrence**, specify the time for the action in **Start Time**.
- If you specified a recurring schedule, you can specify values for **Start Time** and **End Time**. If you specify a start time, the action is performed at this time, and then performs the action based on the recurring schedule. If you specify an end time, the action is not performed after this time.

6. Choose **Create**.

Update a Scheduled Action

If your requirements change, you can update a scheduled action.

To update a scheduled action

1. Open the Amazon EC2 console at https://console.aws.amazon.com/ec2/.

2. On the navigation pane, under **Auto Scaling**, choose **Auto Scaling Groups**.

3. Select your Auto Scaling group.

4. On the **Scheduled Actions** tab, select the scheduled action.

5. Choose **Actions, Edit**.

6. On the **Edit Scheduled Action** page, do the following:

   - Update the size of the group as needed using **Min, Max**, or **Desired Capacity**.
   - Update the specified recurrence as needed.
   - Update the start and end time as needed.
   - Choose **Save**.

Create or Update a Scheduled Action Using the AWS CLI

You can create a schedule for scaling one time only or for scaling on a recurring schedule.

To schedule scaling for one time only
To increase the number of running instances in your Auto Scaling group at a specific time, in "YYYY-MM-DDThh:mm:ssZ" format in UTC, use the following put-scheduled-update-group-action command:

```
1 aws autoscaling put-scheduled-update-group-action --scheduled-action-name ScaleUp --auto-scaling
    -group-name my-asg --start-time "2013-05-12T08:00:00Z" --desired-capacity 3
```

To decrease the number of running instances in your Auto Scaling group at a specific time, in "YYYY-MM-DDThh:mm:ssZ" format in UTC, use the following put-scheduled-update-group-action command:

```
1 aws autoscaling put-scheduled-update-group-action --scheduled-action-name ScaleDown --auto-
    scaling-group-name my-asg --start-time "2013-05-13T08:00:00Z" --desired-capacity 1
```

To schedule scaling on a recurring schedule
You can specify a recurrence schedule, in UTC, using the Cron format. For more information, see the Cron Wikipedia entry.

Use the following put-scheduled-update-group-action command to create a scheduled action that runs at 00:30 hours on the first of January, June, and December each year:

```
1 aws autoscaling put-scheduled-update-group-action --scheduled-action-name scaleup-schedule-year
    --auto-scaling-group-name my-asg --recurrence "30 0 1 1,6,12 0" --desired-capacity 3
```

Delete a Scheduled Action

When you are finished with a scheduled action, you can delete it.

To delete a scheduled action using the console

1. Open the Amazon EC2 console at https://console.aws.amazon.com/ec2/.

2. On the navigation pane, under **Auto Scaling**, choose **Auto Scaling Groups**.

3. Select your Auto Scaling group.

4. On the **Scheduled Actions** tab, select the scheduled action.

5. Choose **Actions**, **Delete**.

6. When prompted for confirmation, choose **Yes, Delete**.

To delete a scheduled action using the AWS CLI

Use the following delete-scheduled-action command:

```
1  aws autoscaling delete-scheduled-action --scheduled-action-name ScaleUp
```

Dynamic Scaling for Amazon EC2 Auto Scaling

When you configure dynamic scaling, you must define how you want to scale in response to changing demand. For example, say you have a web application that currently runs on two instances and you do not want the CPU utilization of the Auto Scaling group to exceed 70 percent. You can configure your Auto Scaling group to scale automatically to meet this need. The policy type determines how the scaling action is performed.

Topics

- Scaling Policy Types
- Target Tracking Scaling Policies for Amazon EC2 Auto Scaling
- Simple and Step Scaling Policies for Amazon EC2 Auto Scaling
- Add a Scaling Policy to an Existing Auto Scaling Group
- Scaling Based on Amazon SQS

Scaling Policy Types

Amazon EC2 Auto Scaling supports the following types of scaling policies:

- **Target tracking scaling**—Increase or decrease the current capacity of the group based on a target value for a specific metric. This is similar to the way that your thermostat maintains the temperature of your home – you select a temperature and the thermostat does the rest.
- **Step scaling**—Increase or decrease the current capacity of the group based on a set of scaling adjustments, known as *step adjustments*, that vary based on the size of the alarm breach.
- **Simple scaling**—Increase or decrease the current capacity of the group based on a single scaling adjustment.

If you are scaling based on a utilization metric that increases or decreases proportionally to the number of instances in an Auto Scaling group, we recommend that you use target tracking scaling policies. Otherwise, we recommend that you use step scaling policies.

Target Tracking Scaling Policies for Amazon EC2 Auto Scaling

Target tracking scaling policies simplify how you configure dynamic scaling. You select a predefined metric or configure a customized metric, and set a target value. Amazon EC2 Auto Scaling creates and manages the CloudWatch alarms that trigger the scaling policy and calculates the scaling adjustment based on the metric and the target value. The scaling policy adds or removes capacity as required to keep the metric at, or close to, the specified target value. In addition to keeping the metric close to the target value, a target tracking scaling policy also adjusts to the fluctuations in the metric due to a fluctuating load pattern and minimizes rapid fluctuations in the capacity of the Auto Scaling group.

For example, you could use target tracking scaling to:

- Configure a target tracking scaling policy to keep the average aggregate CPU utilization of your Auto Scaling group at 50 percent.
- Configure a target tracking scaling policy to keep the request count per target of your Elastic Load Balancing target group at 1000 for your Auto Scaling group.

You can also use target tracking scaling with Application Auto Scaling. For more information, see Target Tracking Scaling Policies in the *Application Auto Scaling User Guide*.

When specifying a customized metric, be aware that not all metrics work for target tracking. The metric must be a valid utilization metric and describe how busy an instance is. The metric value must increase or decrease proportionally to the number of instances in the Auto Scaling group so that the metric data can be used to proportionally scale out or in the number of instances. For example, the CPU utilization of an Auto Scaling group (that is, the Amazon EC2 metric `CPUUtilization` with the dimension `AutoScalingGroupName`) works, if the load on the Auto Scaling group is distributed across the instances. The following metrics do not work:

- The number of requests received by the load balancer fronting the Auto Scaling group (that is, the Elastic Load Balancing metric `RequestCount`), because the number of requests received by the load balancer doesn't change based on the utilization of the Auto Scaling group.
- Load balancer request latency (that is, the Elastic Load Balancing metric `Latency`), because request latency can increase based on increasing utilization, but doesn't necessarily change proportionally.
- The SQS metric `ApproximateNumberOfMessagesVisible`, because the number of messages in a queue may not change proportionally to the size of the Auto Scaling group that processes messages from the queue. However, if the messages are distributed across the instances, a custom metric that measures the number of messages in the queue per instance of the Auto Scaling group would work.

You can have multiple target tracking scaling policies for an Auto Scaling group, provided that each of them is using a different metric. The Auto Scaling group scales based on the policy that provides the largest capacity in the group for both scale in and scale out. This allows you greater flexibility to cover multiple scenarios and ensure that there is always enough capacity to process your application workloads.

You can also optionally disable the scale-in portion of a target tracking scaling policy. This feature provides you with the flexibility to scale in your Auto Scaling group using a different method, for example a different scaling policy type, while using a target tracking scaling policy to scale out your Auto Scaling group.

Considerations

Keep the following considerations in mind:

- A target tracking scaling policy assumes that it should scale out your Auto Scaling group when the specified metric is above the target value. You cannot use a target tracking scaling policy to scale out your Auto Scaling group when the specified metric is below the target value.
- A target tracking scaling policy does not scale your Auto Scaling group when the specified metric has insufficient data. It does not scale in your Auto Scaling group because it does not interpret insufficient data as low utilization. To scale in your Auto Scaling group when the specified metric has insufficient data, create a simple or step scaling policy and have an alarm invoke the scaling policy when it changes

to the `INSUFFICIENT_DATA` state. For example, the metric `RequestCountPerTarget`, which is one of the predefined metrics, has no data points when no requests are routed to the target group. To scale in your Auto Scaling group when no requests are routed to the target group, create a simple or step scaling policy, create an alarm on the metric, and have it invoke the scaling policy when it changes to the `INSUFFICIENT_DATA` state.

- You may see gaps between the target value and the actual metric data points. This is because we act conservatively by rounding up or down when determining how many instances to add or remove. This prevents us from adding an insufficient number of instances or removing too many instances. However, for smaller Auto Scaling groups with fewer instances, the utilization of the group may seem far from the target value. For example, if you set a target value of 50 percent for CPU utilization and your Auto Scaling group then exceeds the target, we might determine that adding 1.5 instances would decrease the CPU utilization to close to 50 percent. Because it is not possible to add 1.5 instances, we round up and add two instances. This might decrease the CPU utilization to a value below 50 percent, but it ensures that your application has enough resources to support it. Similarly, if we determine that removing 1.5 instances increases your CPU utilization to above 50 percent, we remove just one instance. For larger Auto Scaling groups with more instances, the utilization is spread over a larger number of instances. Adding or removing instances causes less of a gap between the target value and the actual metric data points.
- We recommend that you scale on metrics with a 1-minute frequency because that ensures a faster response to utilization changes. Scaling on metrics with a 5-minute frequency can result in slower response time and scaling on stale metric data. By default, Amazon EC2 instances are enabled for basic monitoring, which means metric data for instances is available at 5-minute intervals. You can enable detailed monitoring to get metric data for instances at 1-minute frequency. For more information, see Configure Monitoring for Auto Scaling Instances.
- To ensure application availability, the Auto Scaling group scales out proportionally to the metric as fast as it can, but scales in more gradually.
- Do not edit or delete the CloudWatch alarms that Amazon EC2 Auto Scaling manages for a target tracking scaling policy. The alarms are deleted automatically when you delete the scaling policy.

Create an Auto Scaling Group with Target Tracking Scaling Policies

Use the console to create an Auto Scaling group with a target tracking scaling policy.

To create an Auto Scaling group with scaling based on metrics

1. Open the Amazon EC2 console at https://console.aws.amazon.com/ec2/.

2. On the navigation pane, under **Auto Scaling**, choose **Auto Scaling Groups**.

3. Choose **Create Auto Scaling group**.

4. On the **Create Auto Scaling Group** page, do one of the following:

   - Select **Create an Auto Scaling group from an existing launch configuration**, select an existing launch configuration, and then choose **Next Step**.
   - If you don't have a launch configuration that you'd like to use, choose **Create a new launch configuration** and follow the directions. For more information, see Creating a Launch Configuration.

5. On the **Configure Auto Scaling group details** page, do the following:

   1. For **Group name**, type a name for your Auto Scaling group.

   2. For **Group size**, type the desired capacity for your Auto Scaling group.

   3. If the launch configuration specifies instances that require a VPC, such as T2 instances, you must select a VPC from **Network**. Otherwise, if your AWS account supports EC2-Classic and the instances don't require a VPC, you can select either `Launch info EC2-Classic` or a VPC.

   4. If you selected a VPC in the previous step, select one or more subnets from **Subnet**. If you selected EC2-Classic in the previous step, select one or more Availability Zones from **Availability Zone(s)**.

5. Choose **Next: Configure scaling policies**.

6. On the **Configure scaling policies** page, do the following:

    1. Select **Use scaling policies to adjust the capacity of this group**.

    2. Specify the minimum and maximum size for your Auto Scaling group using the row that begins with **Scale between**. For example, if your group is already at its maximum size, specify a new maximum in order to scale out.

    3. For **Scale Group Size**, specify a scaling policy. You can optionally specify a name for the policy, then choose a value for **Metric type**.

    4. Specify a **Target value** for the metric.

    5. Specify an instance warm-up value for **Instances need**, which allows you to control the time until a newly launched instance can contribute to the CloudWatch metrics.

    6. Check the **Disable scale-in** option to create only a scale-out policy. This allows you to create a separate scale-in policy of a different type if wanted.

    7. Choose **Review**.

    8. On the **Review** page, choose **Create Auto Scaling group**.

Instance Warmup

With target tracking scaling policies, you can specify the number of seconds that it takes for a newly launched instance to warm up. Until its specified warm-up time has expired, an instance is not counted toward the aggregated metrics of the Auto Scaling group.

While scaling out, we do not consider instances that are warming up as part of the current capacity of the group. This ensures that we don't add more instances than you need.

While scaling in, we consider instances that are terminating as part of the current capacity of the group. Therefore, we don't remove more instances from the Auto Scaling group than necessary.

A scale-in activity can't start while a scale-out activity is in progress.

Configure Scaling Policies Using the AWS CLI

Use the AWS CLI as follows to configure target tracking scaling policies for your Auto Scaling group.

Topics

- Step 1: Create an Auto Scaling Group
- Step 2: Create Scaling Policies

Step 1: Create an Auto Scaling Group

Use the following create-auto-scaling-group command to create an Auto Scaling group named `my-asg` using the launch configuration `my-lc`. If you don't have a launch configuration that you'd like to use, you can create one. For more information, see create-launch-configuration.

```
1 aws autoscaling create-auto-scaling-group --auto-scaling-group-name my-asg --launch-
      configuration-name my-lc --max-size 5 --min-size 1 --availability-zones "us-west-2c"
```

Step 2: Create Scaling Policies

You can create scaling policies that tell the Auto Scaling group what to do when the specified conditions change.

Example: target tracking configuration file

The following is an example of a target tracking configuration file, which you should save as `config.json`:

```
1 {
2     "TargetValue": 40.0,
3     "PredefinedMetricSpecification":
4         {
5             "PredefinedMetricType": "ASGAverageCPUUtilization"
6         }
7 }
```

Example: my-scaleout-policy

Use the following put-scaling-policy command, along with the `config.json` file you created previously, to create a scaling policy named **cpu40** that keeps the average CPU utilization of the Auto Scaling group at 40 percent:

```
1 aws autoscaling put-scaling-policy --policy-name cpu40 --auto-scaling-group-name my-asg --policy
    -type TargetTrackingScaling --target-tracking-configuration file://config.json
```

Simple and Step Scaling Policies for Amazon EC2 Auto Scaling

Amazon EC2 Auto Scaling originally supported only simple scaling policies. If you created your scaling policy before target tracking and step policies were introduced, your policy is treated as a simple scaling policy.

We recommend that you use step scaling policies instead of simple scaling policies even if you have a single step adjustment, because we continuously evaluate alarms and do not lock the group during scaling activities or health check replacements. If you are scaling based on a metric that is a utilization metric that increases or decreases proportionally to the number of instances in the Auto Scaling group, we recommend that you use a target tracking scaling policy instead. For more information, see Target Tracking Scaling Policies for Amazon EC2 Auto Scaling.

Simple Scaling Policies

After a scaling activity is started, the policy must wait for the scaling activity or health check replacement to complete and the cooldown period to expire before it can respond to additional alarms. Cooldown periods help to prevent the initiation of additional scaling activities before the effects of previous activities are visible. You can use the default cooldown period associated with your Auto Scaling group, or you can override the default by specifying a cooldown period for your policy. For more information, see Scaling Cooldowns for Amazon EC2 Auto Scaling.

Step Scaling Policies

After a scaling activity is started, the policy continues to respond to additional alarms, even while a scaling activity or health check replacement is in progress. Therefore, all alarms that are breached are evaluated by Amazon EC2 Auto Scaling as it receives the alarm messages. If you are creating a policy to scale out, you can specify the estimated warm-up time that it takes for a newly launched instance to be ready to contribute to the aggregated metrics. For more information, see Instance Warmup.

Note
Amazon EC2 Auto Scaling does not support cooldown periods for step scaling policies. Therefore, you can't specify a cooldown period for these policies and the default cooldown period for the group doesn't apply.

Scaling Adjustment Types

When a step scaling or simple scaling policy is executed, it changes the current capacity of your Auto Scaling group using the scaling adjustment specified in the policy. A scaling adjustment can't change the capacity of the group above the maximum group size or below the minimum group size.

Amazon EC2 Auto Scaling supports the following adjustment types for step scaling and simple scaling:

- **ChangeInCapacity**—Increase or decrease the current capacity of the group by the specified number of instances. A positive value increases the capacity and a negative adjustment value decreases the capacity.

  Example: If the current capacity of the group is 3 instances and the adjustment is 5, then when this policy is performed, there are 5 instances added to the group for a total of 8 instances.

- **ExactCapacity**—Change the current capacity of the group to the specified number of instances. Specify a positive value with this adjustment type.

  Example: If the current capacity of the group is 3 instances and the adjustment is 5, then when this policy is performed, the capacity is set to 5 instances.

- **PercentChangeInCapacity**—Increment or decrement the current capacity of the group by the specified percentage. A positive value increases the capacity and a negative value decreases the capacity. If the resulting value is not an integer, it is rounded as follows:
  - Values greater than 1 are rounded down. For example, `12.7` is rounded to `12`.
  - Values between 0 and 1 are rounded to 1. For example, `.67` is rounded to `1`.
  - Values between 0 and -1 are rounded to -1. For example, `-.58` is rounded to `-1`.
  - Values less than -1 are rounded up. For example, `-6.67` is rounded to `-6`.

  Example: If the current capacity is 10 instances and the adjustment is 10 percent, then when this policy is performed, 1 instance is added to the group for a total of 11 instances.

With **PercentChangeInCapacity**, you can also specify the minimum number of instances to scale (using the `MinAdjustmentMagnitude` parameter or **Add instances in increments of at least** in the console). For example, suppose that you create a policy that adds 25 percent and you specify a minimum increment of 2 instances. If you have an Auto Scaling group with 4 instances and the scaling policy is executed, 25 percent of 4 is 1 instance. However, because you specified a minimum increment of 2, there are 2 instances added.

Step Adjustments

When you create a step scaling policy, you add one or more step adjustments that enable you to scale based on the size of the alarm breach. Each step adjustment specifies a lower bound for the metric value, an upper bound for the metric value, and the amount by which to scale, based on the scaling adjustment type.

There are a few rules for the step adjustments for your policy:

- The ranges of your step adjustments can't overlap or have a gap.
- Only one step adjustment can have a null lower bound (negative infinity). If one step adjustment has a negative lower bound, then there must be a step adjustment with a null lower bound.
- Only one step adjustment can have a null upper bound (positive infinity). If one step adjustment has a positive upper bound, then there must be a step adjustment with a null upper bound.
- The upper and lower bound can't be null in the same step adjustment.
- If the metric value is above the breach threshold, the lower bound is inclusive and the upper bound is exclusive. If the metric value is below the breach threshold, the lower bound is exclusive and the upper bound is inclusive.

Amazon EC2 Auto Scaling applies the aggregation type to the metric data points from all instances. It compares the aggregated metric value against the upper and lower bounds defined by the step adjustments to determine which step adjustment to perform.

If you are using the AWS Management Console, you specify the upper and lower bounds as absolute values. If you are using the API or the CLI, you specify the upper and lower bounds relative to the breach threshold. For example, suppose that you have an alarm with a breach threshold of 50 and a scaling adjustment type of `PercentChangeInCapacity`. You also have scale-out and scale-in policies with the following step adjustments:

Scale out policy
Lower bound
0
10
20
Scale in policy
Lower bound
-10
-20
null

Your group has both a current capacity and a desired capacity of 10 instances. The group maintains its current and desired capacity while the aggregated metric value is greater than 40 and less than 60.

If the metric value gets to 60, the desired capacity of the group increases by 1 instance, to 11 instances, based on the second step adjustment of the scale-out policy (add 10 percent of 10 instances). After the new instance is running and its specified warm-up time has expired, the current capacity of the group increases to 11 instances. If the metric value rises to 70 even after this increase in capacity, the desired capacity of the group increases by another 3 instances, to 14 instances, based on the third step adjustment of the scale-out policy (add 30 percent of 11 instances, 3.3 instances, rounded down to 3 instances).

If the metric value gets to 40, the desired capacity of the group decreases by 1 instance, to 13 instances, based on the second step adjustment of the scale-in policy (remove 10 percent of 14 instances, 1.4 instances, rounded down to 1 instance). If the metric value falls to 30 even after this decrease in capacity, the desired capacity of the group decreases by another 3 instances, to 10 instances, based on the third step adjustment of the scale-in policy (remove 30 percent of 13 instances, 3.9 instances, rounded down to 3 instances).

Instance Warmup

With step scaling policies, you can specify the number of seconds that it takes for a newly launched instance to warm up. Until its specified warm-up time has expired, an instance is not counted toward the aggregated metrics of the Auto Scaling group.

While scaling out, we do not consider instances that are warming up as part of the current capacity of the group. Therefore, multiple alarm breaches that fall in the range of the same step adjustment result in a single scaling activity. This ensures that we don't add more instances than you need. Using the example in the previous section, suppose that the metric gets to 60, and then it gets to 62 while the new instance is still warming up. The current capacity is still 10 instances, so 1 instance is added (10 percent of 10 instances), but the desired capacity of the group is already 11 instances, so we do not increase the desired capacity further. However, if the metric gets to 70 while the new instance is still warming up, we should add 3 instances (30 percent of 10 instances), but the desired capacity of the group is already 11, so we add only 2 instances, for a new desired capacity of 13 instances.

While scaling in, we consider instances that are terminating as part of the current capacity of the group. Therefore, we don't remove more instances from the Auto Scaling group than necessary.

A scale-in activity can't start while a scale-out activity is in progress.

Create an Auto Scaling Group with Step Scaling Policies

You can create a scaling policy that uses CloudWatch alarms to determine when your Auto Scaling group should scale out or scale in. Each CloudWatch alarm watches a single metric and sends messages to Amazon EC2 Auto Scaling when the metric breaches a threshold that you specify in your policy. You can use alarms to monitor any of the metrics that the services in AWS that you're using send to CloudWatch. Or, you can create and monitor your own custom metrics.

When you create a CloudWatch alarm, you can specify an Amazon SNS topic to send an email notification to when the alarm changes state. For more information, see Create Amazon CloudWatch Alarms.

Use the console to create an Auto Scaling group with two scaling policies: a scale-out policy that increases the capacity of the group by 30 percent, and a scale-in policy that decreases the capacity of the group to two instances.

To create an Auto Scaling group with scaling based on metrics

1. Open the Amazon EC2 console at https://console.aws.amazon.com/ec2/.

2. On the navigation pane, under **Auto Scaling**, choose **Auto Scaling Groups**.

3. Choose **Create Auto Scaling group**.

4. On the **Create Auto Scaling Group** page, do one of the following:

   - Select **Create an Auto Scaling group from an existing launch configuration**, select an existing launch configuration, and then choose **Next Step**.
   - If you don't have a launch configuration that you'd like to use, choose **Create a new launch configuration** and follow the directions. For more information, see Creating a Launch Configuration.

5. On the **Configure Auto Scaling group details** page, do the following:

   1. For **Group name**, type a name for your Auto Scaling group.

   2. For **Group size**, type the desired capacity for your Auto Scaling group.

   3. If the launch configuration specifies instances that require a VPC, such as T2 instances, you must select a VPC from **Network**. Otherwise, if your AWS account supports EC2-Classic and the instances don't require a VPC, you can select either `Launch info EC2-Classic` or a VPC.

   4. If you selected a VPC in the previous step, select one or more subnets from **Subnet**. If you selected EC2-Classic in the previous step, select one or more Availability Zones from **Availability Zone(s)**.

   5. Choose **Next: Configure scaling policies**.

6. On the **Configure scaling policies** page, do the following:

   1. Select **Use scaling policies to adjust the capacity of this group**.

   2. Specify the minimum and maximum size for your Auto Scaling group using the row that begins with **Scale between**. For example, if your group is already at its maximum size, you need to specify a new maximum in order to scale out.

      Scale between 1 and 5 instances. These will be the minimum and maximum size of your group.

   3. Specify your scale-out policy under **Increase Group Size**. You can optionally specify a name for the policy, then choose **Add new alarm**.

   4. On the **Create Alarm** page, choose **create topic**. For **Send a notification to**, type a name for the SNS topic. For **With these recipients**, type one or more email addresses to receive notification. If you want, you can replace the default name for your alarm with a custom name. Next, specify the metric and the criteria for the policy. For example, you can leave the default settings for **Whenever** (Average of CPU Utilization). For **Is**, choose `>=` and type 80 percent. For **For at least**, type 1 consecutive period of `5 Minutes`. Choose **Create Alarm**.

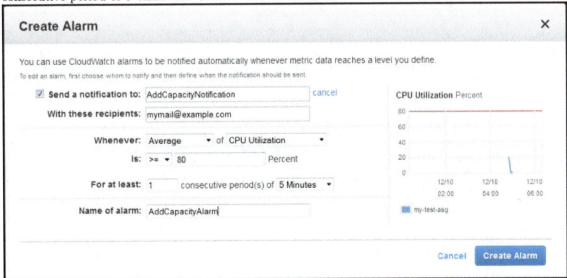

5. For **Take the action**, choose `Add`, type 30 in the next field, and then choose `percent of group`. By default, the lower bound for this step adjustment is the alarm threshold and the upper bound is null (positive infinity).

To add another step adjustment, choose **Add step**. To set a minimum number of instances to scale, update the number field in **Add instances in increments of at least 1 instance(s)**.

(Optional) We recommend that you use the default to create both scaling policies with steps. To create simple scaling policies, choose **Create a simple scaling policy**. For more information, see Scaling Policy Types.

Increase Group Size

Name:	AddCapacity
Execute policy when:	AddCapacityAlarm Edit Remove breaches the alarm threshold: CPUUtilization >= 80 for 300 seconds for the metric dimensions AutoScalingGroupName = my-asg
Take the action:	Add ▾ 30 percent of group ▾ when 80 <= CPUUtilization < +infinity Add step ⓘ Add instances in increments of at least 7 instance(s)
Instances need:	300 seconds to warm up after each step

Create a simple scaling policy ⓘ

6. Specify your scale-in policy under **Decrease Group Size**. You can optionally specify a name for the policy, then choose **Add new alarm**.

7. On the **Create Alarm** page, you can select the same notification that you created for the scale-out policy or create a new one for the scale-in policy. If you want, you can replace the default name for your alarm with a custom name. Keep the default settings for **Whenever** (Average of CPU Utilization). For **Is**, choose `<=` and type 40 percent. For **For at least**, type 1 consecutive period of `5 Minutes`. Choose **Create Alarm**.

8. For **Take the action**, choose `Remove`, type 2 in the next field, and then choose `instances`. By default, the upper bound for this step adjustment is the alarm threshold and the lower bound is null (negative infinity). To add another step adjustment, choose **Add step**.

(Optional) We recommend that you use the default to create both scaling policies with steps. To create simple scaling policies, choose **Create a simple scaling policy**. For more information, see Scaling Policy Types.

Decrease Group Size

Name:	DecreaseCapacity
Execute policy when:	DecreaseCapacityAlarm Edit Remove breaches the alarm threshold: CPUUtilization <= 40 for 300 seconds for the metric dimensions AutoScalingGroupName = my-asg
Take the action:	Remove ▾ 2 instances ▾ when 40 >= CPUUtilization > -infinity Add step ⓘ

Create a simple scaling policy ⓘ

9. Choose **Review**.

10. On the **Review** page, choose **Create Auto Scaling group**.

7. Use the following steps to verify the scaling policies for your Auto Scaling group.

    1. The **Auto Scaling Group creation status** page confirms that your Auto Scaling group was successfully created. Choose **View your Auto Scaling Groups**.

    2. On the **Auto Scaling Groups** page, select the Auto Scaling group that you just created.

    3. On the **Activity History** tab, the **Status** column shows whether your Auto Scaling group has successfully launched instances.

    4. On the **Instances** tab, the **Lifecycle** column contains the state of your instances. It takes a short time for an instance to launch. After the instance starts, its lifecycle state changes to `InService`.

       The **Health Status** column shows the result of the EC2 instance health check on your instance.

    5. On the **Scaling Policies** tab, you can see the policies that you created for the Auto Scaling group.

Configure Scaling Policies Using the AWS CLI

Use the AWS CLI as follows to configure step scaling policies for your Auto Scaling group.

Topics

- Step 1: Create an Auto Scaling Group
- Step 2: Create Scaling Policies
- Step 3: Create CloudWatch Alarms

Step 1: Create an Auto Scaling Group

Use the following create-auto-scaling-group command to create an Auto Scaling group named `my-asg` using the launch configuration `my-lc`. If you don't have a launch configuration that you'd like to use, you can create one. For more information, see create-launch-configuration.

```
1 aws autoscaling create-auto-scaling-group --auto-scaling-group-name my-asg --launch-
      configuration-name my-lc --max-size 5 --min-size 1 --availability-zones "us-west-2c"
```

Step 2: Create Scaling Policies

You can create scaling policies that tell the Auto Scaling group what to do when the specified conditions change.

Example: my-scaleout-policy

Use the following put-scaling-policy command to create a scaling policy named `my-scaleout-policy` with an adjustment type of `PercentChangeInCapacity` that increases the capacity of the group by 30 percent:

```
1 aws autoscaling put-scaling-policy --policy-name my-scaleout-policy --auto-scaling-group-name my
      -asg --scaling-adjustment 30 --adjustment-type PercentChangeInCapacity
```

The output includes the ARN that serves as a unique name for the policy. Later, you can use either the ARN or a combination of the policy name and group name to specify the policy. Store this ARN in a safe place. You need it to create CloudWatch alarms.

```
1 {
2     "PolicyARN": "arn:aws:autoscaling:us-west-2:123456789012:scalingPolicy:ac542982-cbeb
          -4294-891c-a5a941dfa787:autoScalingGroupName/my-asg:policyName/my-scaleout-policy
3 }
```

Example: my-scalein-policy

Use the following put-scaling-policy command to create a scaling policy named `my-scalein-policy` with an adjustment type of `ChangeInCapacity` that decreases the capacity of the group by two instances:

```
1 aws autoscaling put-scaling-policy --policy-name my-scalein-policy --auto-scaling-group-name my-
      asg --scaling-adjustment -2 --adjustment-type ChangeInCapacity
```

The output includes the ARN for the policy. Store this ARN in a safe place. You need it to create CloudWatch alarms.

```
1 {
2    "PolicyARN": "arn:aws:autoscaling:us-west-2:123456789012:scalingPolicy:4ee9e543-86b5-4121-
          b53b-aa4c23b5bbcc:autoScalingGroupName/my-asg:policyName/my-scalein-policy
3 }
```

Step 3: Create CloudWatch Alarms

In step 2, you created scaling policies that provided instructions to the Auto Scaling group about how to scale out and scale in when the conditions that you specify change. In this step, you create alarms by identifying the metrics to watch, defining the conditions for scaling, and then associating the alarms with the scaling policies.

Example: AddCapacity

Use the following CloudWatch put-metric-alarm command to create an alarm that increases the size of the Auto Scaling group when the value of the specified metric breaches 80. For example, you can add capacity when the average CPU usage of all the instances (`CPUUtilization`) increases to 80 percent. To use your own custom metric, specify its name in `--metric-name` and its namespace in `--namespace`.

```
1 aws cloudwatch put-metric-alarm --alarm-name AddCapacity --metric-name CPUUtilization --
      namespace AWS/EC2 --statistic Average --period 120 --threshold 80 --comparison-operator
      GreaterThanOrEqualToThreshold --dimensions "Name=AutoScalingGroupName,Value=my-asg" --
      evaluation-periods 2 --alarm-actions PolicyARN
```

Example: RemoveCapacity

Use the following CloudWatch put-metric-alarm command to create an alarm that decreases the size of the Auto Scaling group when the value of the specified metric breaches 40. For example, you can remove capacity when the average CPU usage of all the instances (`CPUUtilization`) decreases to 40 percent. To use your own custom metric, specify its name in `--metric-name` and its namespace in `--namespace`.

```
1 aws cloudwatch put-metric-alarm --alarm-name RemoveCapacity --metric-name CPUUtilization --
      namespace AWS/EC2 --statistic Average --period 120 --threshold 40 --comparison-operator
      LessThanOrEqualToThreshold --dimensions "Name=AutoScalingGroupName,Value=my-asg" --
      evaluation-periods 2 --alarm-actions PolicyARN
```

Add a Scaling Policy to an Existing Auto Scaling Group

Use the console to add a scaling policy to an existing Auto Scaling group.

To update an Auto Scaling group with scaling based on metrics

1. Open the Amazon EC2 console at https://console.aws.amazon.com/ec2/.

2. On the navigation pane, under **Auto Scaling**, choose **Auto Scaling Groups**.

3. Select the Auto Scaling group.

4. On the **Scaling Policies** tab, choose **Add policy**.

5. If you are adding a target tracking scaling policy, use the following steps. If you are using a simple or step scaling policy, skip to the next step.

   1. For **Name**, type a name for the policy.

   2. Choose a **Metric type** and specify a **Target value** for the metric.

   3. Specify an instance warm-up value for **Instances need**, which allows you to control the amount of time until a newly launched instance can contribute to the CloudWatch metrics.

   4. Check the **Disable scale-in** option if you only want a scale-out policy created. This allows you to create a separate scale-in policy if wanted.

   5. Choose **Create**.

6. If you are using a step scaling policy, do the following:

   1. For **Name**, type a name for the policy, and then choose **Create new alarm**.

   2. On the **Create Alarm** page, choose **create topic**. For **Send a notification to**, type a name for the SNS topic. For **With these recipients**, type one or more email addresses to receive notification. If you want, you can replace the default name for your alarm with a custom name. Next, specify the metric and the criteria for the alarm, using **Whenever**, **Is**, and **For at least**. Choose **Create Alarm**.

   3. Specify the scaling activity for the policy using **Take the action**. By default, the lower bound for this step adjustment is the alarm threshold and the upper bound is null (positive infinity). To add another step adjustment, choose **Add step**.

      (Optional) We recommend that you use the default to create both scaling policies with steps. To create simple scaling policies, choose **Create a simple scaling policy**. For more information, see Scaling Policy Types.

   4. Choose **Create**.

Scaling Based on Amazon SQS

Amazon Simple Queue Service (Amazon SQS) is a scalable message queuing system that stores messages as they travel between various components of your application architecture. Amazon SQS enables web service applications to quickly and reliably queue messages that are generated by one component and consumed by another component. A queue is a temporary repository for messages that are awaiting processing. For more information, see the Amazon Simple Queue Service Developer Guide.

For example, suppose that you have a web app that receives orders from customers. The app runs on EC2 instances in an Auto Scaling group that is configured to handle a typical number of orders. The app places the orders in an Amazon SQS queue until they are picked up for processing, processes the orders, and then sends the processed orders back to the customer. The following diagram illustrates the architecture of this example.

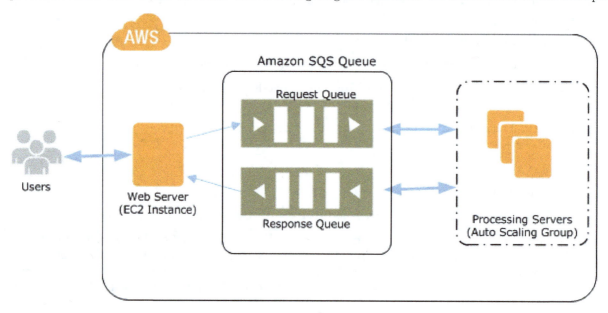

This architecture works well if your order levels remain the same at all times. What happens if your order levels change? You would need to launch additional EC2 instances when the orders increase and terminate the extra EC2 instances when the orders decrease. If your orders increase and decrease on a predictable schedule, you can specify the time and date to perform scaling activities. For more information, see Scheduled Scaling for Amazon EC2 Auto Scaling. Otherwise, you can scale based on criteria, such as the number of messages in your SQS queue. For more information, see Dynamic Scaling for Amazon EC2 Auto Scaling.

Queues provide a convenient mechanism to determine the load on an application. You can use the length of the queue (number of messages available for retrieval from the queue) to determine the load. Because each message in the queue represents a request from a user, measuring the length of the queue is a fair approximation of the load on the application. CloudWatch integrates with Amazon SQS to collect, view, and analyze metrics from SQS queues. You can use the metrics sent by Amazon SQS to determine the length of the SQS queue at any point in time. For a list of all the metrics that Amazon SQS sends to CloudWatch, see Amazon SQS Metrics in the *Amazon Simple Queue Service Developer Guide*.

The following examples create scaling policies that configure your Auto Scaling group to scale based on the number of messages in your SQS queue.

Scaling with Amazon SQS Using the AWS CLI

The following example shows you how to create policies for scaling in and scaling out, plus create, verify, and validate CloudWatch alarms for your scaling policies. It assumes that you already have an SQS queue, an Auto Scaling group, and EC2 instances running the application that uses the SQS queue.

Create the Scaling Policies

You can create scaling policies that tell the Auto Scaling group what to do when the specified conditions change.

To create scaling policies

1. Use the following put-scaling-policy command to create a scale-out policy to increase the Auto Scaling group by one EC2 instance:

```
1 aws autoscaling put-scaling-policy --policy-name my-sqs-scaleout-policy --auto-scaling-
      group-name my-asg --scaling-adjustment 1 --adjustment-type ChangeInCapacity
```

The output includes the Amazon Resource Name (ARN) for the new policy. Store the ARN in a safe place. You need it when you create the CloudWatch alarms.

2. Use the following put-scaling-policy command to create a scale-in policy to decrease the Auto Scaling group by one EC2 instance:

```
1 aws autoscaling put-scaling-policy --policy-name my-sqs-scalein-policy --auto-scaling-group
      -name my-asg --scaling-adjustment -1 --adjustment-type ChangeInCapacity
```

The output includes the ARN for the new policy. Store the ARN in a safe place. You need it when you create the CloudWatch alarms.

Create the CloudWatch Alarms

Next, you create alarms by identifying the metrics to watch, defining the conditions for scaling, and then associating the alarms with the scaling policies that you created in the previous task.

Note
All active SQS queues send metrics to CloudWatch every five minutes. We recommend that you set the alarm `Period` to at least 300 seconds. Setting the alarm `Period` to less than 300 seconds results in the alarm going to the `INSUFFICIENT_DATA` state while waiting for the metrics.

To create CloudWatch alarms

1. Use the following put-metric-alarm command to create an alarm that increases the size of the Auto Scaling group when the number of messages in the queue available for processing (`ApproximateNumberOfMessagesVisible`) increases to three and remains at three or greater for at least five minutes.

```
1 aws cloudwatch put-metric-alarm --alarm-name AddCapacityToProcessQueue --metric-name
      ApproximateNumberOfMessagesVisible --namespace "AWS/SQS" --statistic Average --period
      300 --threshold 3 --comparison-operator GreaterThanOrEqualToThreshold --dimensions Name
      =QueueName,Value=my-queue --evaluation-periods 2 --alarm-actions arn
```

2. Use the following put-metric-alarm command to create an alarm that decreases the size of the Auto Scaling group when the number of messages in the queue available for processing (`ApproximateNumberOfMessagesVisible`) decreases to one and the length remains at one or fewer for at least five minutes.

```
1 aws cloudwatch put-metric-alarm --alarm-name RemoveCapacityFromProcessQueue --metric-name
      ApproximateNumberOfMessagesVisible --namespace "AWS/SQS" --statistic Average --period
      300 --threshold 1 --comparison-operator LessThanOrEqualToThreshold --dimensions Name=
      QueueName,Value=my-queue --evaluation-periods 2 --alarm-actions arn
```

Verify Your Scaling Policies and CloudWatch Alarms

You can verify that your CloudWatch alarms and scaling policies were created.

To verify your CloudWatch alarms
Use the following describe-alarms command:

```
1 aws cloudwatch describe-alarms --alarm-names AddCapacityToProcessQueue
    RemoveCapacityFromProcessQueue
```

To verify your scaling policies
Use the following describe-policies command:

```
1 aws autoscaling describe-policies --auto-scaling-group-name my-asg
```

Test Your Scale Out and Scale In Policies

You can test your scale-out policy by increasing the number of messages in your SQS queue and then verifying that your Auto Scaling group has launched an additional EC2 instance. Similarly, you can test your scale-in policy by decreasing the number of messages in your SQS queue and then verifying that the Auto Scaling group has terminated an EC2 instance.

To test the scale-out policy

1. Follow the steps in Getting Started with Amazon SQS to add messages to your SQS queue. Make sure that you have at least three messages in the queue.

   It takes a few minutes for the SQS queue metric `ApproximateNumberOfmessagesVisible` to invoke the CloudWatch alarm. After the CloudWatch alarm is invoked, it notifies the scaling policy to launch one EC2 instance.

2. Use the following describe-auto-scaling-groups command to verify that the group has launched an instance:

   ```
   1 aws autoscaling describe-auto-scaling-groups --auto-scaling-group-name my-asg
   ```

To test the scale-in policy

1. Follow the steps in Getting Started with Amazon SQS to remove messages from the SQS queue. Make sure that you have no more than one message in the queue.

   It takes a few minutes for the SQS queue metric `ApproximateNumberOfmessagesVisible` to invoke the CloudWatch alarm. After the CloudWatch alarm is invoked, it notifies the scaling policy to terminate one EC2 instance.

2. Use the following describe-auto-scaling-groups command to verify that the group has terminated an instance:

   ```
   1 aws autoscaling describe-auto-scaling-groups --auto-scaling-group-name my-asg
   ```

Scaling Cooldowns for Amazon EC2 Auto Scaling

The cooldown period is a configurable setting for your Auto Scaling group that helps to ensure that it doesn't launch or terminate additional instances before the previous scaling activity takes effect. After the Auto Scaling group dynamically scales using a simple scaling policy, it waits for the cooldown period to complete before resuming scaling activities. When you manually scale your Auto Scaling group, the default is not to wait for the cooldown period, but you can override the default and honor the cooldown period. If an instance becomes unhealthy, the Auto Scaling group does not wait for the cooldown period to complete before replacing the unhealthy instance.

Important
Amazon EC2 Auto Scaling does not support cooldown periods for step scaling policies or scheduled scaling. Application Auto Scaling supports cooldown periods for step scaling policies (see Cooldown Period).

Amazon EC2 Auto Scaling supports both default cooldown periods and scaling-specific cooldown periods.

Topics

- Example: Cooldowns
- Default Cooldowns
- Scaling-Specific Cooldowns
- Cooldowns and Multiple Instances
- Cooldowns and Lifecycle Hooks
- Cooldowns and Spot Instances

Example: Cooldowns

Consider the following scenario: you have a web application running in AWS. This web application consists of three basic tiers: web, application, and database. To make sure that the application always has the resources to meet traffic demands, you create two Auto Scaling groups: one for your web tier and one for your application tier.

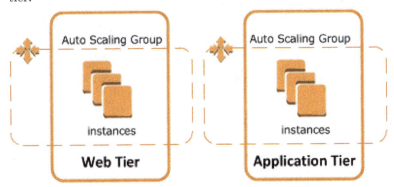

To help ensure that the Auto Scaling group for the application tier has the appropriate number of EC2 instances, create a CloudWatch alarm to scale out whenever the **CPUUtilization** metric for the instances exceeds 90 percent. When the alarm occurs, the Auto Scaling group launches and configures another instance.

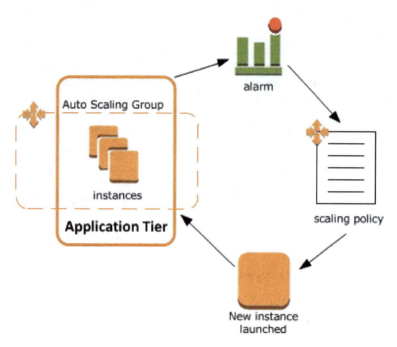

These instances use a configuration script to install and configure software before the instance is put into service. As a result, it takes around two or three minutes from the time the instance launches until it comes in service. The actual time depends on several factors, such as the size of the instance and whether there are startup scripts to complete.

Now a spike in traffic occurs, causing the CloudWatch alarm to fire. When it does, the Auto Scaling group launches an instance to help with the increase in demand. However, there's a problem: the instance takes a couple of minutes to launch. During that time, the CloudWatch alarm could continue to fire, causing the Auto Scaling group to launch another instance each time the alarm fires.

However, with a cooldown period in place, the Auto Scaling group launches an instance and then suspends scaling activities due to simple scaling policies or manual scaling until the specified time elapses. (The default is 300 seconds.) This gives newly launched instances time to start handling application traffic. After the cooldown period expires, any suspended scaling actions resume. If the CloudWatch alarm fires again, the Auto Scaling group launches another instance, and the cooldown period takes effect again. If, however, the additional instance was enough to bring the CPU utilization back down, then the group remains at its current size.

Default Cooldowns

The default cooldown period is applied when you create your Auto Scaling group. Its default value is 300 seconds. This cooldown period automatically applies to any dynamic scaling activities for simple scaling policies, and you can optionally request that it apply to your manual scaling activities.

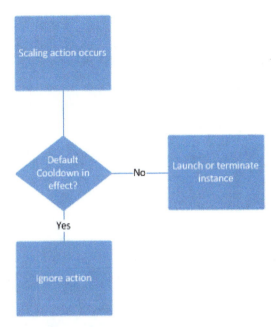

You can configure the default cooldown period when you create the Auto Scaling group, using the AWS Management Console, the create-auto-scaling-group command (AWS CLI), or the CreateAutoScalingGroup API operation.

You can change the default cooldown period at any time, using the AWS Management Console, the update-auto-scaling-group command (AWS CLI), or the UpdateAutoScalingGroup API operation.

Scaling-Specific Cooldowns

In addition to specifying the default cooldown period for your Auto Scaling group, you can create cooldowns that apply to a specific simple scaling policy or manual scaling. A scaling-specific cooldown period overrides the default cooldown period.

One common use for scaling-specific cooldowns is with a scale-in policy—a policy that terminates instances based on a specific criteria or metric. Because this policy terminates instances, Amazon EC2 Auto Scaling needs less time to determine whether to terminate additional instances. The default cooldown period of 300 seconds is too long—you can reduce costs by applying a scaling-specific cooldown period of 180 seconds to the scale-in policy.

You can create a scaling-specific cooldown period using the AWS Management Console, the put-scaling-policy command (AWS CLI), or the PutScalingPolicy API operation.

Cooldowns and Multiple Instances

The preceding sections have provided examples that show how cooldown periods affect Auto Scaling groups when a single instance launches or terminates. However, it is not uncommon for Auto Scaling groups to launch more than one instance at a time. For example, you might choose to have the Auto Scaling group launch three instances when a specific metric threshold is met.

With multiple instances, the cooldown period (either the default cooldown or the scaling-specific cooldown) takes effect starting when the last instance launches.

Cooldowns and Lifecycle Hooks

You can add lifecycle hooks to your Auto Scaling groups. These hooks enable you to control how instances launch and terminate within an Auto Scaling group; you can perform actions on the instance before it is put into service or before it is terminated.

Lifecycle hooks can affect the impact of any cooldown periods configured for the Auto Scaling group, manual scaling, or a simple scaling policy. The cooldown period does not begin until after the instance moves out of the wait state.

Cooldowns and Spot Instances

You can create Auto Scaling groups to use Spot Instances instead of On-Demand or Reserved Instances. The cooldown period begins when the bid for any Spot Instance is successful.

Controlling Which Auto Scaling Instances Terminate During Scale In

With each Auto Scaling group, you control when it adds instances (referred to as *scaling out*) or remove instances (referred to as *scaling in*) from your network architecture. You can scale the size of your group manually by attaching and detaching instances, or you can automate the process through the use of a scaling policy.

When you configure automatic scale in, you must decide which instances should terminate first and set up a termination policy.

You can also use instance protection to prevent specific instances from being terminated during automatic scale in.

Topics

- Default Termination Policy
- Customizing the Termination Policy
- Instance Protection

Default Termination Policy

The default termination policy is designed to help ensure that your network architecture spans Availability Zones evenly. With the default termination policy, the behavior of the Auto Scaling group is as follows:

1. If there are instances in multiple Availability Zones, select the Availability Zone with the most instances and at least one instance that is not protected from scale in. If there is more than one Availability Zone with this number of instances, select the Availability Zone with the instances that use the oldest launch configuration.

2. Determine which unprotected instances in the selected Availability Zone use the oldest launch configuration. If there is one such instance, terminate it.

3. If there are multiple instances that use the oldest launch configuration, determine which unprotected instances are closest to the next billing hour. (This helps you maximize the use of your EC2 instances and manage your Amazon EC2 usage costs.) If there is one such instance, terminate it.

4. If there is more than one unprotected instance closest to the next billing hour, select one of these instances at random.

The following flow diagram illustrates how the default termination policy works.

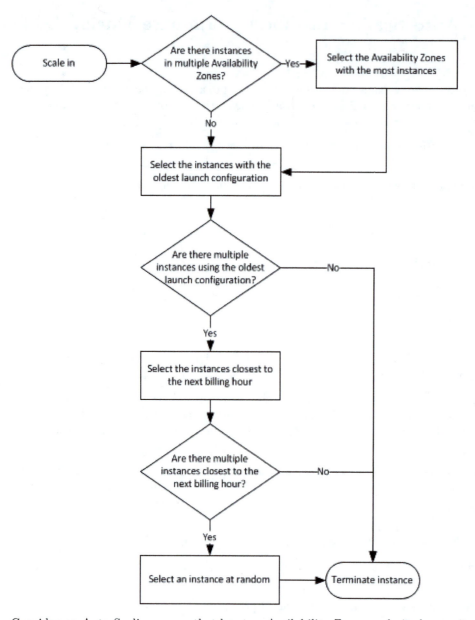

Consider an Auto Scaling group that has two Availability Zones, a desired capacity of two instances, and scaling policies that increase and decrease the number of instances by 1 when certain thresholds are met. The two instances in this group are distributed as follows.

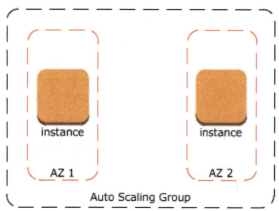

When the threshold for the scale-out policy is met, the policy takes effect and the Auto Scaling group launches a new instance. The Auto Scaling group now has three instances, distributed as follows.

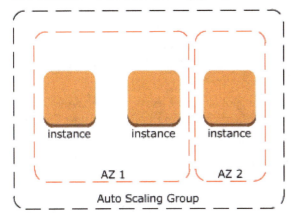

When the threshold for the scale-in policy is met, the policy takes effect and the Auto Scaling group terminates one of the instances. If you did not assign a specific termination policy to the group, it uses the default termination policy. It selects the Availability Zone with two instances, and terminates the instance launched from the oldest launch configuration. If the instances were launched from the same launch configuration, then the Auto Scaling group selects the instance that is closest to the next billing hour and terminates it.

Customizing the Termination Policy

The default termination policy assigned to an Auto Scaling group is typically sufficient for most situations. However, you have the option of replacing the default policy with a customized one.

When you customize the termination policy, if one Availability Zone has more instances than the other Availability Zones that are used by the group, then your termination policy is applied to the instances from the imbalanced Availability Zone. If the Availability Zones used by the group are balanced, then the termination policy is applied across all the Availability Zones for the group.

Amazon EC2 Auto Scaling supports the following custom termination policies:

- `OldestInstance`. Terminate the oldest instance in the group. This option is useful when you're upgrading the instances in the Auto Scaling group to a new EC2 instance type. You can gradually replace instances of the old type with instances of the new type.
- `NewestInstance`. Terminate the newest instance in the group. This policy is useful when you're testing a new launch configuration but don't want to keep it in production.
- `OldestLaunchConfiguration`. Terminate instances that have the oldest launch configuration. This policy is useful when you're updating a group and phasing out the instances from a previous configuration.
- `ClosestToNextInstanceHour`. Terminate instances that are closest to the next billing hour. This policy helps you maximize the use of your instances and manage your Amazon EC2 usage costs.
- `Default`. Terminate instances according to the default termination policy. This policy is useful when you have more than one scaling policy for the group.

To customize a termination policy using the console

1. Open the Amazon EC2 console at https://console.aws.amazon.com/ec2/.

2. On the navigation pane, choose **Auto Scaling Groups**.

3. Select the Auto Scaling group.

4. For **Actions**, choose **Edit**.

5. On the **Details** tab, locate **Termination Policies**. Choose one or more termination policies. If you choose multiple policies, list them in the order that you would like them to apply. If you use the `Default`

policy, make it the last one in the list.

6. Choose **Save**.

To customize a termination policy using the AWS CLI
Use one of the following commands:

- create-auto-scaling-group
- update-auto-scaling-group

You can use these policies individually, or combine them into a list of policies. For example, use the following command to update an Auto Scaling group to use the `OldestLaunchConfiguration` policy first and then use the `ClosestToNextInstanceHour` policy:

```
1  aws autoscaling update-auto-scaling-group --auto-scaling-group-name my-asg --termination-
       policies "OldestLaunchConfiguration,ClosestToNextInstanceHour"
```

If you use the `Default` termination policy, make it the last one in the list of termination policies. For example, `--termination-policies "OldestLaunchConfiguration,Default"`.

Instance Protection

To control whether an Auto Scaling group can terminate a particular instance when scaling in, use instance protection. You can enable the instance protection setting on an Auto Scaling group or an individual Auto Scaling instance. When the Auto Scaling group launches an instance, it inherits the instance protection setting of the Auto Scaling group. You can change the instance protection setting for an Auto Scaling group or an Auto Scaling instance at any time.

Instance protection starts when the instance state is `InService`. If you detach an instance that is protected from termination, its instance protection setting is lost. When you attach the instance to the group again, it inherits the current instance protection setting of the group.

If all instances in an Auto Scaling group are protected from termination during scale in and a scale in event occurs, its desired capacity is decremented. However, the Auto Scaling group can't terminate the required number of instances until their instance protection settings are disabled.

Instance protection does not protect Auto Scaling instances from the following:

- Manual termination through the Amazon EC2 console, the `terminate-instances` command, or the `TerminateInstances` action. To protect Auto Scaling instances from manual termination, enable termination protection. For more information, see Enabling Termination Protection in the *Amazon EC2 User Guide for Linux Instances*.
- Health check replacement if the instance fails health checks.
- Spot Instance interruption.

Topics

- Enable Instance Protection for a Group
- Modify the Instance Protection Setting for a Group
- Modify the Instance Protection Setting for an Instance

Enable Instance Protection for a Group

You can enable instance protection when you create an Auto Scaling group. By default, instance protection is disabled.

To enable instance protection using the console
When you create the Auto Scaling group, on the **Configure Auto Scaling group details** page, under **Advanced Details**, select the `Protect From Scale In` option from **Instance Protection**.

106

▼ Advanced Details

Load Balancing ⓘ	You currently don't have any load balancers Learn about Elastic Load Balancing	
Health Check Grace Period ⓘ	[300] seconds	
Monitoring ⓘ	Amazon EC2 Detailed Monitoring metrics, which are provided at 1 minute frequency, are not enabled for the launch configuration my-lc. Instances launched from it will use Basic Monitoring metrics, provided at 5 minute frequency. Learn more	
Instance Protection ⓘ	Protect From Scale In	

To enable instance protection using the AWS CLI
Use the following create-auto-scaling-group command to enable instance protection:

```
1 aws autoscaling create-auto-scaling-group --auto-scaling-group-name my-asg --new-instances-
    protected-from-scale-in ...
```

Modify the Instance Protection Setting for a Group

You can enable or disable the instance protection setting for an Auto Scaling group.

To change the instance protection setting for a group using the console

1. Open the Amazon EC2 console at https://console.aws.amazon.com/ec2/.

2. On the navigation pane, choose **Auto Scaling Groups**.

3. Select the Auto Scaling group.

4. On the **Details** tab, choose **Edit**.

5. For **Instance Protection**, select `Protect From Scale In`.

Instance Protection
```
|
Protect From Scale In
```

6. Choose **Save**.

To change the instance protection setting for a group using the AWS CLI
Use the following update-auto-scaling-group command to enable instance protection for the specified Auto Scaling group:

```
1 aws autoscaling update-auto-scaling-group --auto-scaling-group-name my-asg --new-instances-
    protected-from-scale-in
```

Use the following command to disable instance protection for the specified group:

```
1 aws autoscaling update-auto-scaling-group --auto-scaling-group-name my-asg --no-new-instances-
    protected-from-scale-in
```

Modify the Instance Protection Setting for an Instance

By default, an instance gets its instance protection setting from its Auto Scaling group. However, you can enable or disable instance protection for an instance at any time.

To change the instance protection setting for an instance using the console

1. Open the Amazon EC2 console at https://console.aws.amazon.com/ec2/.

2. On the navigation pane, choose **Auto Scaling Groups**.

3. Select the Auto Scaling group.

4. On the **Instances** tab, select the instance.

5. To enable instance protection, choose **Actions, Instance Protection, Set Scale In Protection**. When prompted, choose **Set Scale In Protection**.

6. To disable instance protection, choose **Actions, Instance Protection, Remove Scale In Protection**. When prompted, choose **Remove Scale In Protection**.

To change the instance protection setting for an instance using the AWS CLI

Use the following set-instance-protection command to enable instance protection for the specified instance:

```
1 aws autoscaling set-instance-protection --instance-ids i-5f2e8a0d --auto-scaling-group-name my-
    asg --protected-from-scale-in
```

Use the following command to disable instance protection for the specified instance:

```
1 aws autoscaling set-instance-protection --instance-ids i-5f2e8a0d --auto-scaling-group-name my-
    asg --no-protected-from-scale-in
```

Amazon EC2 Auto Scaling Lifecycle Hooks

Lifecycle hooks enable you to perform custom actions by pausing instances as an Auto Scaling group launches or terminates them. For example, while your newly launched instance is paused, you could install or configure software on it.

Each Auto Scaling group can have multiple lifecycle hooks. However, there is a limit on the number of hooks per Auto Scaling group. For more information, see Auto Scaling Limits.

Topics

- How Lifecycle Hooks Work
- Considerations When Using Lifecycle Hooks
- Prepare for Notifications
- Add Lifecycle Hooks
- Complete the Lifecycle Hook
- Test the Notification

How Lifecycle Hooks Work

After you add lifecycle hooks to your Auto Scaling group, they work as follows:

1. Responds to scale out events by launching instances and scale in events by terminating instances.

2. Puts the instance into a wait state (`Pending:Wait` or `Terminating:Wait`). The instance is paused until either you continue or the timeout period ends.

3. You can perform a custom action using one or more of the following options:

   - Define a CloudWatch Events target to invoke a Lambda function when a lifecycle action occurs. The Lambda function is invoked when Amazon EC2 Auto Scaling submits an event for a lifecycle action to CloudWatch Events. The event contains information about the instance that is launching or terminating, and a token that you can use to control the lifecycle action.
   - Define a notification target for the lifecycle hook. Amazon EC2 Auto Scaling sends a message to the notification target. The message contains information about the instance that is launching or terminating, and a token that you can use to control the lifecycle action.
   - Create a script that runs on the instance as the instance starts. The script can control the lifecycle action using the ID of the instance on which it runs.

4. By default, the instance remains in a wait state for one hour, and then the Auto Scaling group continues the launch or terminate process (`Pending:Proceed` or `Terminating:Proceed`). If you need more time, you can restart the timeout period by recording a heartbeat. If you finish before the timeout period ends, you can complete the lifecycle action, which continues the launch or termination process.

The following illustration shows the transitions between instance states in this process:

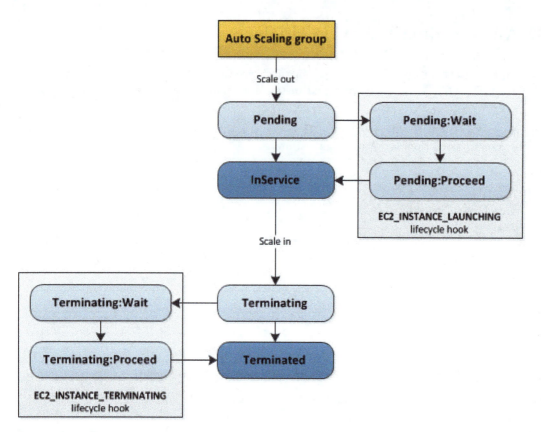

For more information about the complete lifecycle of instances in an Auto Scaling group, see Auto Scaling Lifecycle.

Considerations When Using Lifecycle Hooks

Adding lifecycle hooks to your Auto Scaling group gives you greater control over how instances launch and terminate. Here are some things to consider when adding a lifecycle hook to your Auto Scaling group, to help ensure that the group continues to perform as expected.

Topics

- Keeping Instances in a Wait State
- Cooldowns and Custom Actions
- Health Check Grace Period
- Lifecycle Action Result
- Spot Instances

Keeping Instances in a Wait State

Instances can remain in a wait state for a finite period of time. The default is 1 hour (3600 seconds). You can adjust this time in the following ways:

- Set the heartbeat timeout for the lifecycle hook when you create the lifecycle hook. With the put-lifecycle-hook command, use the `--heartbeat-timeout` parameter. With the PutLifecycleHook operation, use the `HeartbeatTimeout` parameter.
- Continue to the next state if you finish before the timeout period ends, using the complete-lifecycle-action command or the CompleteLifecycleAction operation.
- Restart the timeout period by recording a heartbeat, using the record-lifecycle-action-heartbeat command or the RecordLifecycleActionHeartbeat operation. This increments the heartbeat timeout by the timeout

110

value specified when you created the lifecycle hook. For example, if the timeout value is 1 hour, and you call this command after 30 minutes, the instance remains in a wait state for an additional hour, or a total of 90 minutes.

The maximum amount of time that you can keep an instance in a wait state is 48 hours or 100 times the heartbeat timeout, whichever is smaller.

Cooldowns and Custom Actions

When an Auto Scaling group launches or terminates an instance due to a simple scaling policy, a cooldown takes effect. The cooldown period helps ensure that the Auto Scaling group does not launch or terminate more instances than needed.

Consider an Auto Scaling group with a lifecycle hook that supports a custom action at instance launch. When the application experiences an increase in demand, the group launches instances to add capacity. Because there is a lifecycle hook, the instance is put into the `Pending:Wait` state, which means that it is not available to handle traffic yet. When the instance enters the wait state, scaling actions due to simple scaling policies are suspended. When the instance enter the `InService` state, the cooldown period starts. When the cooldown period expires, any suspended scaling actions resume.

Health Check Grace Period

If you add a lifecycle hook to perform actions as your instances launch, the health check grace period does not start until you complete the lifecycle hook and the instance enters the `InService` state.

Lifecycle Action Result

At the conclusion of a lifecycle hook, the result is either `ABANDON` or `CONTINUE`.

If the instance is launching, `CONTINUE` indicates that your actions were successful, and that the instance can be put into service. Otherwise, `ABANDON` indicates that your custom actions were unsuccessful, and that the instance can be terminated.

If the instance is terminating, both `ABANDON` and `CONTINUE` allow the instance to terminate. However, `ABANDON` stops any remaining actions, such as other lifecycle hooks, while `CONTINUE` allows any other lifecycle hooks to complete.

Spot Instances

You can use lifecycle hooks with Spot Instances. However, a lifecycle hook does not prevent an instance from terminating due to a change in the Spot Price, which can happen at any time. In addition, when a Spot Instance terminates, you must still complete the lifecycle action (using the complete-lifecycle-action command or the CompleteLifecycleAction operation).

Prepare for Notifications

You can optionally configure notifications when the instance enters a wait state, which enables you to perform a custom action. You can use Amazon CloudWatch Events, Amazon SNS, or Amazon SQS to receive the notifications. Choose whichever option you prefer.

Alternatively, if you have a script that configures your instances when they launch, you do not need to receive notification when the lifecycle action occurs. If you are not doing so already, update your script to retrieve the instance ID of the instance from the instance metadata. For more information, see Retrieving Instance Metadata.

Topics

- Receive Notification Using CloudWatch Events
- Receive Notification Using Amazon SNS
- Receive Notification Using Amazon SQS

Receive Notification Using CloudWatch Events

You can use CloudWatch Events to set up a target to invoke a Lambda function when a lifecycle action occurs.

To set up notifications using CloudWatch Events

1. Create a Lambda function using the steps in Create a Lambda Function and note its Amazon Resource Name (ARN). For example, `arn:aws:lambda:us-west-2:123456789012:function:my-function`.

2. Create a CloudWatch Events rule that matches the lifecycle action using the following put-rule command:

```
1 aws events put-rule --name my-rule --event-pattern file://pattern.json --state ENABLED
```

The `pattern.json` for an instance launch lifecycle action is:

```
1 {
2   "source": [ "aws.autoscaling" ],
3   "detail-type": [ "EC2 Instance-launch Lifecycle Action" ]
4 }
```

The `pattern.json` for an instance terminate lifecycle action is:

```
1 {
2   "source": [ "aws.autoscaling" ],
3   "detail-type": [ "EC2 Instance-terminate Lifecycle Action" ]
4 }
```

3. Grant the rule permission to invoke your Lambda function using the following add-permission command. This command trusts the CloudWatch Events service principal (`events.amazonaws.com`) and scopes permissions to the specified rule.

```
1 aws lambda add-permission --function-name LogScheduledEvent --statement-id my-scheduled-
    event --action 'lambda:InvokeFunction' --principal events.amazonaws.com --source-arn
    arn:aws:events:us-east-1:123456789012:rule/my-scheduled-rule
```

4. Create a target that invokes your Lambda function when the lifecycle action occurs, using the following put-targets command:

```
1 aws events put-targets --rule my-rule --targets Id=1,Arn=arn:aws:lambda:us-west
    -2:123456789012:function:my-function
```

5. When the Auto Scaling group responds to a scale-out or scale-in event, it puts the instance in a wait state. While the instance is in a wait state, the Lambda function is invoked. For more information about the event data, see Auto Scaling Events.

Receive Notification Using Amazon SNS

You can use Amazon SNS to set up a notification target to receive notifications when a lifecycle action occurs.

To set up notifications using Amazon SNS

1. Create the target using Amazon SNS. For more information, see Create a Topic in the *Amazon Simple Notification Service Developer Guide*. Note the ARN of the target (for example, `arn:aws:sns:us-west-2:123456789012:my-sns-topic`).

2. Create an IAM role to grant Amazon EC2 Auto Scaling permissions to access your notification target, using the steps in Creating a Role to Delegate Permissions to an AWS Service in the *IAM User Guide*. When prompted to select a role type, select **AWS Service Roles, AutoScaling Notification Access**. Note the ARN of the role. For example, `arn:aws:iam::123456789012:role/my-notification-role`.

3. When the Auto Scaling group responds to a scale-out or scale in event, it puts the instance in a wait state. While the instance is in a wait state, a message is published to the notification target. The message includes the following event data:

   - **LifecycleActionToken** — The lifecycle action token.
   - **AccountId** — The AWS account ID.
   - **AutoScalingGroupName** — The name of the Auto Scaling group.
   - **LifecycleHookName** — The name of the lifecycle hook.
   - **EC2InstanceId** — The ID of the EC2 instance.
   - **LifecycleTransition** — The lifecycle hook type.

For example:

```
1 Service: AWS Auto Scaling
2 Time: 2016-09-30T20:42:11.305Z
3 RequestId: 18b2ec17-3e9b-4c15-8024-ff2e8ce8786a
4 LifecycleActionToken: 71514b9d-6a40-4b26-8523-05e7ee35fa40
5 AccountId: 123456789012
6 AutoScalingGroupName: my-asg
7 LifecycleHookName: my-hook
8 EC2InstanceId: i-0598c7d356eba48d7
9 LifecycleTransition: autoscaling:EC2_INSTANCE_LAUNCHING
10 NotificationMetadata: null
```

Receive Notification Using Amazon SQS

You can use Amazon SQS to set up a notification target to receive notifications when a lifecycle action occurs.

Important
FIFO queues are not compatible with lifecycle hooks.

To set up notifications using Amazon SQS

1. Create the target using Amazon SQS. For more information, see Getting Started with Amazon SQS in the *Amazon Simple Queue Service Developer Guide*. Note the ARN of the target.

2. Create an IAM role to grant Amazon EC2 Auto Scaling permission to access your notification target, using the steps in Creating a Role to Delegate Permissions to an AWS Service in the *IAM User Guide*. When prompted to select a role type, select **AWS Service Roles, AutoScaling Notification Access**. Note the ARN of the role. For example, `arn:aws:iam::123456789012:role/my-notification-role`.

3. When the Auto Scaling group responds to a scale-out or scale-in event, it puts the instance in a wait state. While the instance is in a wait state, a message is published to the notification target.

Add Lifecycle Hooks

You can create lifecycle hooks using the put-lifecycle-hook command.

To perform an action on scale out, use the following command:

```
1 aws autoscaling put-lifecycle-hook --lifecycle-hook-name my-hook --auto-scaling-group-name my-
    asg --lifecycle-transition autoscaling:EC2_INSTANCE_LAUNCHING
```

To perform an action on scale in, use the following command instead:

```
1 aws autoscaling put-lifecycle-hook --lifecycle-hook-name my-hook --auto-scaling-group-name my-
    asg --lifecycle-transition autoscaling:EC2_INSTANCE_TERMINATING
```

(Optional) To receive notifications using Amazon SNS or Amazon SQS, there are additional options. For example, add the following options to specify an SNS topic as the notification target:

```
1 --notification-target-arn arn:aws:sns:us-west-2:123456789012:my-sns-topic --role-arn arn:aws:iam
    ::123456789012:role/my-notification-role
```

The topic receives a test notification with the following key-value pair:

```
1 "Event": "autoscaling:TEST_NOTIFICATION"
```

Complete the Lifecycle Hook

When an Auto Scaling group responds to a scale out or scale in event, it puts the instance in a wait state and sends any notifications. It continues the launch or terminate process after you complete the lifecycle hook.

To complete a lifecycle hook

1. While the instance is in a wait state, you can perform a custom action. For more information, see Prepare for Notifications.

2. If you need more time to complete the custom action, use the record-lifecycle-action-heartbeat command to restart the timeout period and keep the instance in a wait state. You can specify the lifecycle action token you received in the previous step, as shown in the following command:

```
1 aws autoscaling record-lifecycle-action-heartbeat --lifecycle-action-token bcd2f1b8-9a78-44
    d3-8a7a-4dd07d7cf635 --lifecycle-hook-name my-launch-hook --auto-scaling-group-name my-
    asg
```

Alternatively, you can specify the ID of the instance you retrieved in the previous step, as shown in the following command:

```
1 aws autoscaling record-lifecycle-action-heartbeat --instance-id i-1a2b3c4d --lifecycle-hook
    -name my-launch-hook --auto-scaling-group-name my-asg
```

3. If you finish the custom action before the timeout period ends, use the complete-lifecycle-action command so that the Auto Scaling group can continue launching or terminating the instance. You can specify the lifecycle action token, as shown in the following command:

```
1 aws autoscaling complete-lifecycle-action --lifecycle-action-result CONTINUE --lifecycle-
    action-token bcd2f1b8-9a78-44d3-8a7a-4dd07d7cf635 --lifecycle-hook-name my-launch-hook
    --auto-scaling-group-name my-asg
```

Alternatively, you can specify the ID of the instance, as shown in the following command:

```
1 aws autoscaling complete-lifecycle-action --lifecycle-action-result CONTINUE --instance-id
    i-1a2b3c4d --lifecycle-hook-name my-launch-hook --auto-scaling-group-name my-asg
```

Test the Notification

To generate a notification for a launch event, update the Auto Scaling group by increasing the desired capacity of the Auto Scaling group by 1. You receive a notification within a few minutes after instance launch.

To change the desired capacity using the console

1. Open the Amazon EC2 console at https://console.aws.amazon.com/ec2/.

2. On the navigation pane, under **Auto Scaling**, choose **Auto Scaling Groups**.

3. Select your Auto Scaling group.

4. On the **Details** tab, choose **Edit**.

5. For **Desired**, increase the current value by 1. If this value exceeds **Max**, you must also increase the value of **Max** by 1.

6. Choose **Save**.

7. After a few minutes, you'll receive notification for the event. If you do not need the additional instance that you launched for this test, you can decrease **Desired** by 1. After a few minutes, you'll receive notification for the event.

Temporarily Removing Instances from Your Auto Scaling Group

You can put an instance that is in the `InService` state into the `Standby` state, update or troubleshoot the instance, and then return the instance to service. Instances that are on standby are still part of the Auto Scaling group, but they do not actively handle application traffic.

Important
You are billed for instances that are in a standby state.

For example, you can change the launch configuration for an Auto Scaling group at any time, and any subsequent instances that the Auto Scaling group launches use this configuration. However, the Auto Scaling group does not update the instances that are currently in service. You can either terminate these instances and let the Auto Scaling group replace them, or you can put the instances on standby, update the software, and then put the instances back in service.

Topics

- How the Standby State Works
- Health Status of an Instance in a Standby State
- Temporarily Remove an Instance Using the AWS Management Console
- Temporarily Remove an Instance Using the AWS CLI

How the Standby State Works

The standby state works as follows to help you temporarily remove an instance from your Auto Scaling group:

1. You put the instance into the standby state. The instance remains in this state until you exit the standby state.

2. If there is a load balancer or target group attached to your Auto Scaling group, the instance is deregistered from the load balancer or target group.

3. By default, the desired capacity of your Auto Scaling group is decremented when you put an instance on standby. This prevents the launch of an additional instance while you have this instance on standby. Alternatively, you can specify that the capacity is not decremented. This causes the Auto Scaling group to launch an additional instance to replace the one on standby.

4. You can update or troubleshoot the instance.

5. You return the instance to service by exiting the standby state.

6. After you put an instance that was on standby back in service, the desired capacity is incremented. If you did not decrement the capacity when you put the instance on standby, the Auto Scaling group detects that you have more instances than you need, and applies the termination policy in effect to reduce the size of the group. For more information, see Controlling Which Auto Scaling Instances Terminate During Scale In.

7. If there is a load balancer or target group attached to your Auto Scaling group, the instance is registered with the load balancer or target group.

The following illustration shows the transitions between instance states in this process:

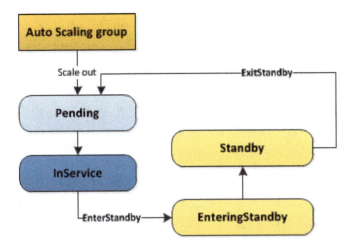

For more information about the complete lifecycle of instances in an Auto Scaling group, see Auto Scaling Lifecycle.

Health Status of an Instance in a Standby State

Amazon EC2 Auto Scaling does not perform health checks on instances that are in a standby state. While the instance is in a standby state, its health status reflects the status that it had before you put it on standby. Amazon EC2 Auto Scaling does not perform a health check on the instance until you put it back in service.

For example, if you put a healthy instance on standby and then terminate it, Amazon EC2 Auto Scaling continues to report the instance as healthy. If you return the terminated instance to service, Amazon EC2 Auto Scaling performs a health check on the instance, determines that it is unhealthy, and launches a replacement instance.

Temporarily Remove an Instance Using the AWS Management Console

The following procedure demonstrates the general process for updating an instance that is currently in service.

To temporarily remove an instance using the console

1. Open the Amazon EC2 console at https://console.aws.amazon.com/ec2/.

2. On the navigation pane, under **Auto Scaling**, choose **Auto Scaling Groups**.

3. Select the Auto Scaling group.

4. On the **Instances** tab, select the instance.

5. Choose **Actions, Set to Standby**.

6. On the **Set to Standby** page, select the check box to launch a replacement instance. Leave it unchecked to decrement the desired capacity. Choose **Set to Standby**.

7. You can update or troubleshoot your instance as needed. When you have finished, continue with the next step to return the instance to service.

8. Select the instance, choose **Actions, Set to InService**. On the **Set to InService** page, choose **Set to InService**.

Temporarily Remove an Instance Using the AWS CLI

The following procedure demonstrates the general process for updating an instance that is currently in service.

To temporarily remove an instance using the AWS CLI

1. Use the following describe-auto-scaling-instances command to identify the instance to update:

```
1 aws autoscaling describe-auto-scaling-instances
```

The following is an example response:

```
1 {
2     "AutoScalingInstances": [
3         {
4             "AvailabilityZone": "us-west-2a",
5             "InstanceId": "i-5b73d709",
6             "AutoScalingGroupName": "my-asg",
7             "HealthStatus": "HEALTHY",
8             "LifecycleState": "InService",
9             "LaunchConfigurationName": "my-lc"
10         },
11         ...
12     ]
13 }
```

2. Move the instance into a Standby state using the following enter-standby command. The --should-decrement-desired-capacity option decreases the desired capacity so that the Auto Scaling group does not launch a replacement instance.

```
1 aws autoscaling enter-standby --instance-ids i-5b73d709 --auto-scaling-group-name my-asg --
    should-decrement-desired-capacity
```

The following is an example response:

```
1 {
2     "Activities": [
3         {
4             "Description": "Moving EC2 instance to Standby: i-5b73d709",
5             "AutoScalingGroupName": "my-asg",
6             "ActivityId": "3b1839fe-24b0-40d9-80ae-bcd883c2be32",
7             "Details": "{\"Availability Zone\":\"us-west-2a\"}",
8             "StartTime": "2014-12-15T21:31:26.150Z",
9             "Progress": 50,
10            "Cause": "At 2014-12-15T21:31:26Z instance i-5b73d709 was moved to standby
11                in response to a user request, shrinking the capacity from 4 to 3.",
12            "StatusCode": "InProgress"
13         }
14     ]
15 }
```

3. (Optional) Verify that the instance is in Standby using the following describe-auto-scaling-instances command:

```
1 aws autoscaling describe-auto-scaling-instances --instance-ids i-5b73d709
```

The following is an example response. Notice that the status of the instance is now Standby.

```
1 {
2     "AutoScalingInstances": [
3         {
4             "AvailabilityZone": "us-west-2a",
5             "InstanceId": "i-5b73d709",
6             "AutoScalingGroupName": "my-asg",
```

```
7              "HealthStatus": "HEALTHY",
8              "LifecycleState": "Standby",
9              "LaunchConfigurationName": "my-lc"
10         }
11     ]
12 }
```

4. You can update or troubleshoot your instance as needed. When you have finished, continue with the next step to return the instance to service.

5. Put the instance back in service using the following exit-standby command:

```
1 aws autoscaling exit-standby --instance-ids i-5b73d709 --auto-scaling-group-name my-asg
```

The following is an example response:

```
1 {
2     "Activities": [
3         {
4              "Description": "Moving EC2 instance out of Standby: i-5b73d709",
5              "AutoScalingGroupName": "my-asg",
6              "ActivityId": "db12b166-cdcc-4c54-8aac-08c5935f8389",
7              "Details": "{\"Availability Zone\":\"us-west-2a\"}",
8              "StartTime": "2014-12-15T21:46:14.678Z",
9              "Progress": 30,
10             "Cause": "At 2014-12-15T21:46:14Z instance i-5b73d709 was moved out of standby
                  in
11                 response to a user request, increasing the capacity from 3 to 4.",
12             "StatusCode": "PreInService"
13         }
14     ]
15 }
```

6. (Optional) Verify that the instance is back in service using the following describe-auto-scaling-instances command:

```
1 aws autoscaling describe-auto-scaling-instances --instance-ids i-5b73d709
```

The following is an example response. Notice that the status of the instance is InService.

```
1 {
2     "AutoScalingInstances": [
3         {
4              "AvailabilityZone": "us-west-2a",
5              "InstanceId": "i-5b73d709",
6              "AutoScalingGroupName": "my-asg",
7              "HealthStatus": "HEALTHY",
8              "LifecycleState": "InService",
9              "LaunchConfigurationName": "my-lc"
10         }
11     ]
12 }
```

Suspending and Resuming Scaling Processes

You can suspend and then resume one or more of the scaling processes for your Auto Scaling group. This can be useful when you want to investigate a configuration problem or other issue with your web application and then make changes to your application, without triggering the scaling processes.

Amazon EC2 Auto Scaling can suspend processes for Auto Scaling groups that repeatedly fail to launch instances. This is known as an *administrative suspension*, and most commonly applies to Auto Scaling groups that have been trying to launch instances for over 24 hours but have not succeeded in launching any instances. You can resume processes suspended for administrative reasons.

Topics

- Scaling Processes
- Suspend and Resume Processes Using the Console
- Suspend and Resume Processes Using the AWS CLI

Scaling Processes

Amazon EC2 Auto Scaling supports the following scaling processes:

`Launch`
Adds a new EC2 instance to the group, increasing its capacity.
If you suspend `Launch`, this disrupts other processes. For example, you can't return an instance in a standby state to service if the `Launch` process is suspended, because the group can't scale.

`Terminate`
Removes an EC2 instance from the group, decreasing its capacity.
If you suspend `Terminate`, this disrupts other processes.

`HealthCheck`
Checks the health of the instances. Amazon EC2 Auto Scaling marks an instance as unhealthy if Amazon EC2 or Elastic Load Balancing tells Amazon EC2 Auto Scaling that the instance is unhealthy. This process can override the health status of an instance that you set manually.

`ReplaceUnhealthy`
Terminates instances that are marked as unhealthy and later creates new instances to replace them. This process works with the `HealthCheck` process, and uses both the `Terminate` and `Launch` processes.

`AZRebalance`
Balances the number of EC2 instances in the group across the Availability Zones in the region. If you remove an Availability Zone from your Auto Scaling group or an Availability Zone otherwise becomes unhealthy or unavailable, the scaling process launches new instances in an unaffected Availability Zone before terminating the unhealthy or unavailable instances. When the unhealthy Availability Zone returns to a healthy state, the scaling process automatically redistributes the instances evenly across the Availability Zones for the group. For more information, see Rebalancing Activities.
If you suspend `AZRebalance` and a scale out or scale in event occurs, the scaling process still tries to balance the Availability Zones. For example, during scale out, it launches the instance in the Availability Zone with the fewest instances.
If you suspend the `Launch` process, `AZRebalance` neither launches new instances nor terminates existing instances. This is because `AZRebalance` terminates instances only after launching the replacement instances. If you suspend the `Terminate` process, your Auto Scaling group can grow up to ten percent larger than its maximum size, because this is allowed temporarily during rebalancing activities. If the scaling process cannot terminate instances, your Auto Scaling group could remain above its maximum size until you resume the `Terminate` process.

`AlarmNotification`
Accepts notifications from CloudWatch alarms that are associated with the group.

120

If you suspend `AlarmNotification`, Amazon EC2 Auto Scaling does not automatically execute policies that would be triggered by an alarm. If you suspend `Launch` or `Terminate`, it would not be able to execute scale-out or scale-in policies, respectively.

`ScheduledActions`
Performs scheduled actions that you create.
If you suspend `Launch` or `Terminate`, scheduled actions that involve launching or terminating instances are affected.

`AddToLoadBalancer`
Adds instances to the attached load balancer or target group when they are launched.
If you suspend `AddToLoadBalancer`, Amazon EC2 Auto Scaling launches the instances but does not add them to the load balancer or target group. If you resume the `AddToLoadBalancer` process, it resumes adding instances to the load balancer or target group when they are launched. However, it does not add the instances that were launched while this process was suspended. You must register those instances manually.

Suspend and Resume Processes Using the Console

You can suspend and resume individual processes using the AWS Management Console.

To suspend and resume processes using the console

1. Open the Amazon EC2 console at https://console.aws.amazon.com/ec2/.

2. On the navigation pane, under **Auto Scaling**, choose **Auto Scaling Groups**.

3. Select the Auto Scaling group.

4. On the **Details** tab, choose **Edit**.

5. For **Suspended Processes**, select the process to suspend.

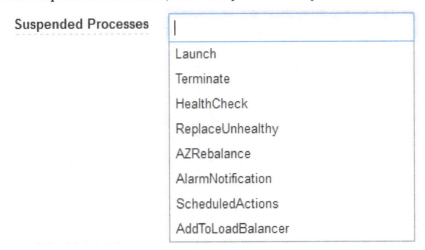

To resume a suspended process, remove it from **Suspended Processes**.

6. Choose **Save**.

Suspend and Resume Processes Using the AWS CLI

You can suspend and resume individual processes or all processes.

To suspend a process

Use the suspend-processes command with the `--scaling-processes` option as follows:

```
1 aws autoscaling suspend-processes --auto-scaling-group-name my-asg --scaling-processes
    AlarmNotification
```

To suspend all processes

Use the suspend-processes command as follows (omitting the `--scaling-processes` option):

```
1 aws autoscaling suspend-processes --auto-scaling-group-name my-asg
```

To resume a suspended process

Use the resume-processes command as follows:

```
1 aws autoscaling resume-processes --auto-scaling-group-name my-asg --scaling-processes
    AlarmNotification
```

To resume all suspended processes

Use the resume-processes command as follows (omitting the `--scaling-processes` option):

```
1 aws autoscaling resume-processes --auto-scaling-group-name my-asg
```

Monitoring Your Auto Scaling Instances and Groups

You can use the following features to monitor your Auto Scaling instances and groups.

Health checks
Auto Scaling periodically performs health checks on the instances in your Auto Scaling group and identifies any instances that are unhealthy. You can configure Auto Scaling to determine the health status of an instance using Amazon EC2 status checks, Elastic Load Balancing health checks, or custom health checks. For more information, see Health Checks for Auto Scaling Instances.

CloudWatch metrics
Auto Scaling publishes data points to Amazon CloudWatch about your Auto Scaling groups. CloudWatch enables you to retrieve statistics about those data points as an ordered set of time-series data, known as *metrics*. You can use these metrics to verify that your system is performing as expected. For more information, see Monitoring Your Auto Scaling Groups and Instances Using Amazon CloudWatch.

CloudWatch Events
Auto Scaling can submit events to Amazon CloudWatch Events when your Auto Scaling groups launch or terminate instances, or when a lifecycle action occurs. This enables you to invoke a Lambda function when the event occurs. For more information, see Getting CloudWatch Events When Your Auto Scaling Group Scales.

SNS notifications
Auto Scaling can send Amazon SNS notifications when your Auto Scaling groups launch or terminate instances. For more information, see Getting SNS Notifications When Your Auto Scaling Group Scales.

CloudTrail logs
AWS CloudTrail enables you to keep track of the calls made to the Auto Scaling API by or on behalf of your AWS account. CloudTrail stores the information in log files in the Amazon S3 bucket that you specify. You can use these log files to monitor activity of your Auto Scaling groups by determining which requests were made, the source IP addresses where the requests came from, who made the request, when the request was made, and so on. For more information, see Logging Amazon EC2 Auto Scaling API Calls By Using AWS CloudTrail.

Health Checks for Auto Scaling Instances

The health status of an Auto Scaling instance is either healthy or unhealthy. After an instance is fully configured and passes the initial health checks, it is considered healthy by Auto Scaling and enters the `InService` state. Auto Scaling periodically performs health checks on the instances in your Auto Scaling group and identifies any instances that are unhealthy. After Auto Scaling marks an instance as unhealthy, it is scheduled for replacement. For more information, see Replacing Unhealthy Instances.

Instance Health Status

Auto Scaling determines the health status of an instance using one or more of the following:

- Status checks provided by Amazon EC2 (systems status checks and instance status checks. For more information, see Status Checks for Your Instances in the *Amazon EC2 User Guide for Linux Instances*.
- Health checks provided by Elastic Load Balancing. For more information, see Health Checks for Your Target Groups in the *User Guide for Application Load Balancers* or Configure Health Checks for Your Classic Load Balancer in the *User Guide for Classic Load Balancers*.
- Custom health checks.

By default, Auto Scaling health checks use the results of the EC2 status checks to determine the health status of an instance. Auto Scaling marks an instance as unhealthy if its instance fails one or more of the status checks.

If you attached a load balancer or target group to your Auto Scaling group, you can configure Auto Scaling to mark an instance as unhealthy if Elastic Load Balancing reports the instance as `OutOfService`. If connection draining is enabled for your load balancer, Auto Scaling waits for in-flight requests to complete or the maximum timeout to expire, whichever comes first, before terminating instances due to a scaling event or health check replacement. For more information, see Using ELB Health Checks with Auto Scaling.

Health Check Grace Period

Frequently, an Auto Scaling instance that has just come into service needs to warm up before it can pass the Auto Scaling health check. Auto Scaling waits until the health check grace period ends before checking the health status of the instance. While the EC2 status checks and ELB health checks can complete before the health check grace period expires, Auto Scaling does not act on them until the health check grace period expires. To provide ample warm-up time for your instances, ensure that the health check grace period covers the expected startup time for your application. Note that if you add a lifecycle hook to perform actions as your instances launch, the health check grace period does not start until the lifecycle hook is completed and the instance enters the `InService` state.

Custom Health Checks

If you have custom health checks, you can send the information from your health checks to Auto Scaling so that Auto Scaling can use this information. For example, if you determine that an instance is not functioning as expected, you can set the health status of the instance to `Unhealthy`. The next time that Auto Scaling performs a health check on the instance, it will determine that the instance is unhealthy and then launch a replacement instance.

Use the following set-instance-health command to set the health state of the specified instance to `Unhealthy`:

```
1 aws autoscaling set-instance-health --instance-id i-123abc45d --health-status Unhealthy
```

Use the following `describe-auto-scaling-groups` command to verify that the instance state is `Unhealthy`:

```
1 aws autoscaling describe-auto-scaling-groups --auto-scaling-group-names my-asg
```

The following is an example response that shows that the health status of the instance is `Unhealthy` and that the instance is terminating:

```
1  {
2      "AutoScalingGroups": [
3          {
4              ....
5              "Instances": [
6                  {
7                      "InstanceId": "i-123abc45d",
8                      "AvailabilityZone": "us-west-2a",
9                      "HealthStatus": "Unhealthy",
10                     "LifecycleState": "Terminating",
11                     "LaunchConfigurationName": "my-lc"
12                 },
13                 ...
14             ]
15         }
16     ]
17 }
```

Monitoring Your Auto Scaling Groups and Instances Using Amazon CloudWatch

Amazon CloudWatch enables you to retrieve statistics as an ordered set of time-series data, known as metrics. You can use these metrics to verify that your system is performing as expected.

Amazon EC2 sends metrics to CloudWatch that describe your Auto Scaling instances. These metrics are available for any EC2 instance, not just those in an Auto Scaling group. For more information, see Instance Metrics in the *Amazon EC2 User Guide for Linux Instances.*

Auto Scaling groups can send metrics to CloudWatch that describe the group itself. You must enable these metrics.

Topics

- Auto Scaling Group Metrics
- Dimensions for Auto Scaling Group Metrics
- Enable Auto Scaling Group Metrics
- Configure Monitoring for Auto Scaling Instances
- View CloudWatch Metrics
- Create Amazon CloudWatch Alarms

Auto Scaling Group Metrics

The `AWS/AutoScaling` namespace includes the following metrics.

Metric	Description
GroupMinSize	The minimum size of the Auto Scaling group.
GroupMaxSize	The maximum size of the Auto Scaling group.
GroupDesiredCapacity	The number of instances that the Auto Scaling group attempts to maintain.
GroupInServiceInstances	The number of instances that are running as part of the Auto Scaling group. This metric does not include instances that are pending or terminating.
GroupPendingInstances	The number of instances that are pending. A pending instance is not yet in service. This metric does not include instances that are in service or terminating.
GroupStandbyInstances	The number of instances that are in a `Standby` state. Instances in this state are still running but are not actively in service.
GroupTerminatingInstances	The number of instances that are in the process of terminating. This metric does not include instances that are in service or pending.
GroupTotalInstances	The total number of instances in the Auto Scaling group. This metric identifies the number of instances that are in service, pending, and terminating.

Dimensions for Auto Scaling Group Metrics

To filter the metrics for your Auto Scaling group by group name, use the `AutoScalingGroupName` dimension.

Enable Auto Scaling Group Metrics

When you enable Auto Scaling group metrics, Auto Scaling sends sampled data to CloudWatch every minute.

To enable group metrics using the console

1. Open the Amazon EC2 console at https://console.aws.amazon.com/ec2/.

2. In the navigation pane, choose **Auto Scaling Groups**.

3. Select your Auto Scaling group.

4. On the **Monitoring** tab, for **Auto Scaling Metrics**, choose **Enable Group Metrics Collection**. If you don't see this option, select **Auto Scaling** for **Display**.

To disable group metrics using the console

1. Open the Amazon EC2 console at https://console.aws.amazon.com/ec2/.

2. In the navigation pane, choose **Auto Scaling Groups**.

3. Select your Auto Scaling group.

4. On the **Monitoring** tab, for **Auto Scaling Metrics**, choose **Disable Group Metrics Collection**. If you don't see this option, select **Auto Scaling** for **Display**.

To enable group metrics using the AWS CLI

Enable one or more group metrics using the enable-metrics-collection command. For example, the following command enables the GroupDesiredCapacity metric.

```
1 aws autoscaling enable-metrics-collection --auto-scaling-group-name my-asg --metrics
    GroupDesiredCapacity --granularity "1Minute"
```

If you omit the --metrics option, all metrics are enabled.

```
1 aws autoscaling enable-metrics-collection --auto-scaling-group-name my-asg --granularity "1
    Minute"
```

To disable group metrics using the AWS CLI

Use the disable-metrics-collection command. For example, the following command disables all Auto Scaling group metrics:

```
1 aws autoscaling disable-metrics-collection --auto-scaling-group-name my-asg
```

Configure Monitoring for Auto Scaling Instances

By default, basic monitoring is enabled when you create a launch configuration using the AWS Management Console and detailed monitoring is enabled when you create a launch configuration using the AWS CLI or an API.

If you have an Auto Scaling group and need to change which type of monitoring is enabled for your Auto Scaling instances, you must create a new launch configuration and update the Auto Scaling group to use this launch configuration. After that, the instances that the Auto Scaling group launches will use the updated monitoring type. Note that existing instances in the Auto Scaling group continue to use the previous monitoring type. You can terminate these instances so that Auto Scaling replaces them, or update each instance individually using the monitor-instances and unmonitor-instances.

If you have CloudWatch alarms associated with your Auto Scaling group, use the put-metric-alarm command to update each alarm so that its period matches the monitoring type (300 seconds for basic monitoring and 60 seconds for detailed monitoring). If you change from detailed monitoring to basic monitoring but do not update your alarms to match the five-minute period, they continue to check for statistics every minute and might find no data available for as many as four out of every five periods.

To configure CloudWatch monitoring using the console

When you create the launch configuration using the AWS Management Console, on the **Configure Details** page, select **Enable CloudWatch detailed monitoring**. Otherwise, basic monitoring is enabled. For more information, see Creating a Launch Configuration.

To configure CloudWatch monitoring using the AWS CLI

Use the create-launch-configuration command with the `--instance-monitoring` option. Set this option to `true` to enable detailed monitoring or `false` to enable basic monitoring.

```
1 --instance-monitoring Enabled=true
```

View CloudWatch Metrics

You can view the CloudWatch metrics for your Auto Scaling groups and instances using the Amazon EC2 console. These metrics are displayed as monitoring graphs.

Alternatively, you can view these metrics using the CloudWatch console.

To view metrics using the Amazon EC2 console

1. Open the Amazon EC2 console at https://console.aws.amazon.com/ec2/.

2. In the navigation pane, choose **Auto Scaling Groups**.

3. Select your Auto Scaling group.

4. Choose the **Monitoring** tab.

5. (Optional) To filter the results by time, select a time range from **Showing data for**.

6. To view the metrics for your groups, for **Display**, choose **Auto Scaling**. To get a larger view of a single metric, select its graph. The following metrics are available for groups:

- Minimum Group Size — `GroupMinSize`
- Maximum Group Size — `GroupMaxSize`
- Desired Capacity — `GroupDesiredCapacity`
- In Service Instances — `GroupInServiceInstances`
- Pending Instances — `GroupPendingInstances`
- Standby Instances — `GroupStandbyInstances`
- Terminating Instances — `GroupTerminatingInstances`
- Total Instances — `GroupTotalInstances`

7. To view metrics for your instances, for **Display**, choose **EC2**. To get a larger view of a single metric, select its graph. The following metrics are available for instances:

- CPU Utilization — `CPUUtilization`
- Disk Reads — `DiskReadBytes`
- Disk Read Operations — `DiskReadOps`
- Disk Writes — `DiskWriteBytes`
- Disk Write Operations — `DiskWriteOps`
- Network In — `NetworkIn`
- Network Out — `NetworkOut`
- Status Check Failed (Any) — `StatusCheckFailed`
- Status Check Failed (Instance) — `StatusCheckFailed_Instance`
- Status Check Failed (System) — `StatusCheckFailed_System`

To view metrics using the CloudWatch console
For more information, see Aggregate Statistics by Auto Scaling Group.

To view CloudWatch metrics using the AWS CLI
To view all metrics for all your Auto Scaling groups, use the following list-metrics command:

```
1 aws cloudwatch list-metrics --namespace "AWS/AutoScaling"
```

To view the metrics for a single Auto Scaling group, specify the `AutoScalingGroupName` dimension as follows:

```
1 aws cloudwatch list-metrics --namespace "AWS/AutoScaling" --dimensions Name=AutoScalingGroupName
  ,Value=my-asg
```

To view a single metric for all your Auto Scaling groups, specify the name of the metric as follows:

```
1 aws cloudwatch list-metrics --namespace "AWS/AutoScaling" --metric-name GroupDesiredCapacity
```

Create Amazon CloudWatch Alarms

A CloudWatch *alarm* is an object that monitors a single metric over a specific period. A metric is a variable that you want to monitor, such as average CPU usage of the EC2 instances, or incoming network traffic from many different EC2 instances. The alarm changes its state when the value of the metric breaches a defined range and maintains the change for a specified number of periods.

An alarm has three possible states:

- `OK`— The value of the metric remains within the range that you've specified.
- `ALARM`— The value of the metric is out of the range that you've specified for a specified time duration.
- `INSUFFICIENT_DATA`— The metric is not yet available or there is not enough data available to determine the alarm state.

When the alarm changes to the `ALARM` state and remains in that state for a number of periods, it invokes one or more actions. The actions can be a message sent to an Auto Scaling group to change the desired capacity of the group.

You configure an alarm by identifying the metrics to monitor. For example, you can configure an alarm to watch over the average CPU usage of the EC2 instances in an Auto Scaling group.

To create a CloudWatch alarm

1. Open the CloudWatch console at https://console.aws.amazon.com/cloudwatch/.

2. On the navigation pane, choose **Alarms**.

3. Choose **Create Alarm**.

4. Choose the **EC2 Metrics** category.

5. (Optional) You can filter the results. To see the instance metrics, choose **Per-Instance Metrics**. To see the Auto Scaling group metrics, choose **By Auto Scaling Group**.

6. Select a metric, and then choose **Next**.

7. Specify a threshold for the alarm and the action to take.

   For more information, see Creating CloudWatch Alarms in the *Amazon CloudWatch User Guide*.

8. Choose **Create Alarm**.

Getting CloudWatch Events When Your Auto Scaling Group Scales

When you use Auto Scaling to scale your applications automatically, it is useful to know when Auto Scaling is launching or terminating the EC2 instances in your Auto Scaling group. You can configure Auto Scaling to send events to Amazon CloudWatch Events whenever your Auto Scaling group scales.

For more information, see the Amazon CloudWatch Events User Guide.

Topics

- Auto Scaling Events
- Create a Lambda Function
- Route Events to Your Lambda Function

Auto Scaling Events

Auto Scaling supports sending events to CloudWatch Events when the following events occur:

- EC2 Instance-launch Lifecycle Action
- EC2 Instance Launch Successful
- EC2 Instance Launch Unsuccessful
- EC2 Instance-terminate Lifecycle Action
- EC2 Instance Terminate Successful
- EC2 Instance Terminate Unsuccessful

EC2 Instance-launch Lifecycle Action

Auto Scaling moved an instance to a `Pending:Wait` state due to a lifecycle hook.

Event Data
The following is example data for this event.

```
1  {
2    "version": "0",
3    "id": "12345678-1234-1234-1234-123456789012",
4    "detail-type": "EC2 Instance-launch Lifecycle Action",
5    "source": "aws.autoscaling",
6    "account": "123456789012",
7    "time": "yyyy-mm-ddThh:mm:ssZ",
8    "region": "us-west-2",
9    "resources": [
10     "auto-scaling-group-arn"
11   ],
12   "detail": {
13     "LifecycleActionToken": "87654321-4321-4321-4321-210987654321",
14     "AutoScalingGroupName": "my-asg",
15     "LifecycleHookName": "my-lifecycle-hook",
16     "EC2InstanceId": "i-1234567890abcdef0",
17     "LifecycleTransition": "autoscaling:EC2_INSTANCE_LAUNCHING",
18     "NotificationMetadata": "additional-info"
19   }
20 }
```

EC2 Instance Launch Successful

Auto Scaling successfully launched an instance.

Event Data

The following is example data for this event.

```
1  {
2      "version": "0",
3      "id": "12345678-1234-1234-1234-123456789012",
4      "detail-type": "EC2 Instance Launch Successful",
5      "source": "aws.autoscaling",
6      "account": "123456789012",
7      "time": "yyyy-mm-ddThh:mm:ssZ",
8      "region": "us-west-2",
9      "resources": [
10         "auto-scaling-group-arn",
11         "instance-arn"
12     ],
13     "detail": {
14         "StatusCode": "InProgress",
15         "Description": "Launching a new EC2 instance: i-12345678",
16         "AutoScalingGroupName": "my-auto-scaling-group",
17         "ActivityId": "87654321-4321-4321-4321-210987654321",
18         "Details": {
19             "Availability Zone": "us-west-2b",
20             "Subnet ID": "subnet-12345678"
21         },
22         "RequestId": "12345678-1234-1234-1234-123456789012",
23         "StatusMessage": "",
24         "EndTime": "yyyy-mm-ddThh:mm:ssZ",
25         "EC2InstanceId": "i-1234567890abcdef0",
26         "StartTime": "yyyy-mm-ddThh:mm:ssZ",
27         "Cause": "description-text",
28     }
29 }
```

EC2 Instance Launch Unsuccessful

Auto Scaling failed to launch an instance.

Event Data

The following is example data for this event.

```
1  {
2      "version": "0",
3      "id": "12345678-1234-1234-1234-123456789012",
4      "detail-type": "EC2 Instance Launch Unsuccessful",
5      "source": "aws.autoscaling",
6      "account": "123456789012",
7      "time": "yyyy-mm-ddThh:mm:ssZ",
8      "region": "us-west-2",
9      "resources": [
10         "auto-scaling-group-arn",
11         "instance-arn"
```

```
12      ],
13      "detail": {
14          "StatusCode": "Failed",
15          "AutoScalingGroupName": "my-auto-scaling-group",
16          "ActivityId": "87654321-4321-4321-4321-210987654321",
17          "Details": {
18              "Availability Zone": "us-west-2b",
19              "Subnet ID": "subnet-12345678"
20          },
21          "RequestId": "12345678-1234-1234-1234-123456789012",
22          "StatusMessage": "message-text",
23          "EndTime": "yyyy-mm-ddThh:mm:ssZ",
24          "EC2InstanceId": "i-1234567890abcdef0",
25          "StartTime": "yyyy-mm-ddThh:mm:ssZ",
26          "Cause": "description-text",
27      }
28 }
```

EC2 Instance-terminate Lifecycle Action

Auto Scaling moved an instance to a `Terminating:Wait` state due to a lifecycle hook.

Event Data
The following is example data for this event.

```
1 {
2   "version": "0",
3   "id": "12345678-1234-1234-1234-123456789012",
4   "detail-type": "EC2 Instance-terminate Lifecycle Action",
5   "source": "aws.autoscaling",
6   "account": "123456789012",
7   "time": "yyyy-mm-ddThh:mm:ssZ",
8   "region": "us-west-2",
9   "resources": [
10     "auto-scaling-group-arn"
11   ],
12   "detail": {
13     "LifecycleActionToken":"87654321-4321-4321-4321-210987654321",
14     "AutoScalingGroupName":"my-asg",
15     "LifecycleHookName":"my-lifecycle-hook",
16     "EC2InstanceId":"i-1234567890abcdef0",
17     "LifecycleTransition":"autoscaling:EC2_INSTANCE_TERMINATING"
18   }
19 }
```

EC2 Instance Terminate Successful

Auto Scaling successfully terminated an instance.

Event Data
The following is example data for this event.

```
1 {
2   "version": "0",
```

```
3     "id": "12345678-1234-1234-1234-123456789012",
4     "detail-type": "EC2 Instance Terminate Successful",
5     "source": "aws.autoscaling",
6     "account": "123456789012",
7     "time": "yyyy-mm-ddThh:mm:ssZ",
8     "region": "us-west-2",
9     "resources": [
10      "auto-scaling-group-arn",
11      "instance-arn"
12    ],
13    "detail": {
14        "StatusCode": "InProgress",
15        "Description": "Terminating EC2 instance: i-12345678",
16        "AutoScalingGroupName": "my-auto-scaling-group",
17        "ActivityId": "87654321-4321-4321-4321-210987654321",
18        "Details": {
19            "Availability Zone": "us-west-2b",
20            "Subnet ID": "subnet-12345678"
21        },
22        "RequestId": "12345678-1234-1234-1234-123456789012",
23        "StatusMessage": "",
24        "EndTime": "yyyy-mm-ddThh:mm:ssZ",
25        "EC2InstanceId": "i-1234567890abcdef0",
26        "StartTime": "yyyy-mm-ddThh:mm:ssZ",
27        "Cause": "description-text",
28    }
29 }
```

EC2 Instance Terminate Unsuccessful

Auto Scaling failed to terminate an instance.

Event Data
The following is example data for this event.

```
1  {
2     "version": "0",
3     "id": "12345678-1234-1234-1234-123456789012",
4     "detail-type": "EC2 Instance Terminate Unsuccessful",
5     "source": "aws.autoscaling",
6     "account": "123456789012",
7     "time": "yyyy-mm-ddThh:mm:ssZ",
8     "region": "us-west-2",
9     "resources": [
10      "auto-scaling-group-arn",
11      "instance-arn"
12    ],
13    "detail": {
14        "StatusCode": "Failed",
15        "AutoScalingGroupName": "my-auto-scaling-group",
16        "ActivityId": "87654321-4321-4321-4321-210987654321",
17        "Details": {
18            "Availability Zone": "us-west-2b",
19            "Subnet ID": "subnet-12345678"
20        },
```

```
21      "RequestId": "12345678-1234-1234-1234-123456789012",
22      "StatusMessage": "message-text",
23      "EndTime": "yyyy-mm-ddThh:mm:ssZ",
24      "EC2InstanceId": "i-1234567890abcdef0",
25      "StartTime": "yyyy-mm-ddThh:mm:ssZ",
26      "Cause": "description-text",
27    }
28 }
```

Create a Lambda Function

Use the following procedure to create a Lambda function to handle an Auto Scaling event.

To create a Lambda function

1. Open the AWS Lambda console at https://console.aws.amazon.com/lambda/.

2. If you are new to Lambda, you see a welcome page; choose **Get Started Now**; otherwise, choose **Create a Lambda function**.

3. On the **Select blueprint** page, type hello-world for **Filter**, and then select the **hello-world** blueprint.

4. On the **Configure triggers** page, choose **Next**.

5. On the **Configure function** page, do the following:

    1. Type a name and description for the Lambda function.

    2. Edit the code for the Lambda function. For example, the following code simply logs the event:

    ```
    1 console.log('Loading function');
    2
    3 exports.handler = function(event, context) {
    4     console.log("AutoScalingEvent()");
    5     console.log("Event data:\n" + JSON.stringify(event, null, 4));
    6     context.succeed("...");
    7 };
    ```

    3. For **Role**, choose **Choose an existing role** if you have an existing role that you'd like to use, and then choose your role from **Existing role**. Alternatively, to create a new role, choose one of the other options for **Role** and then follow the directions.

    4. (Optional) For **Advanced settings**, make any changes that you need.

    5. Choose **Next**.

6. On the **Review** page, choose **Create function**.

Route Events to Your Lambda Function

Use the following procedure to route Auto Scaling events to your Lambda function.

To route events to your Lambda function

1. Open the CloudWatch console at https://console.aws.amazon.com/cloudwatch/.

2. On the navigation pane, choose **Events**.

3. Choose **Create rule**.

4. For **Event selector**, choose **Auto Scaling** as the event source. By default, the rule applies to all Auto Scaling events for all of your Auto Scaling groups. Alternatively, you can select specific events or a specific Auto Scaling group.

5. For **Targets**, choose **Add target**. Choose **Lambda function** as the target type, and then select your Lambda function.

6. Choose **Configure details**.

7. For **Rule definition**, type a name and description for your rule.

8. Choose **Create rule**.

To test your rule, change the size of your Auto Scaling group. If you used the example code for your Lambda function, it logs the event to CloudWatch Logs.

To test your rule

1. Open the Amazon EC2 console at https://console.aws.amazon.com/ec2/.

2. On the navigation pane, choose **Auto Scaling Groups**, and then select your Auto Scaling group.

3. On the **Details** tab, choose **Edit**.

4. Change the value of **Desired**, and then choose **Save**.

5. Open the CloudWatch console at https://console.aws.amazon.com/cloudwatch/.

6. On the navigation pane, choose **Logs**.

7. Select the log group for your Lambda function (for example, ***/aws/lambda/***my-function).

8. Select a log stream to view the event data. The data is displayed, similar to the following:

Event Data
```
▼ 2016-02-22T17:48:20.778Z ea1fjqinxq6pwo9d Loading function
▼ START RequestId: 7560439b-d98c-11e5-932d-f52757e7aee0 Version: $LATEST
▼ 2016-02-22T17:48:20.813Z 7560439b-d98c-11e5-932d-f52757e7aee0 AutoScalingEvent()
▼ 2016-02-22T17:48:20.814Z 7560439b-d98c-11e5-932d-f52757e7aee0 Event data:
{
    "version": "0",
    "id": "df9b0c8c-89c8-4748-92cb-ac68a9029ada",
    "detail-type": "EC2 Instance Launch Successful",
    "source": "aws.autoscaling",
```

Getting SNS Notifications When Your Auto Scaling Group Scales

When you use Auto Scaling to scale your applications automatically, it is useful to know when Auto Scaling is launching or terminating the EC2 instances in your Auto Scaling group. Amazon SNS coordinates and manages the delivery or sending of notifications to subscribing clients or endpoints. You can configure Auto Scaling to send an SNS notification whenever your Auto Scaling group scales.

Amazon SNS can deliver notifications as HTTP or HTTPS POST, email (SMTP, either plain-text or in JSON format), or as a message posted to an Amazon SQS queue. For more information, see What Is Amazon SNS in the *Amazon Simple Notification Service Developer Guide*.

For example, if you configure your Auto Scaling group to use the `autoscaling:EC2_INSTANCE_TERMINATE` notification type, and your Auto Scaling group terminates an instance, it sends an email notification. This email contains the details of the terminated instance, such as the instance ID and the reason that the instance was terminated.

Tip
If you prefer, you can use Amazon CloudWatch Events to configure a target to invoke a Lambda function when your Auto Scaling group scales or when a lifecycle action occurs. For more information, see Getting CloudWatch Events When Your Auto Scaling Group Scales.

Topics

- SNS Notifications
- Configure Amazon SNS
- Configure Your Auto Scaling Group to Send Notifications
- Test the Notification Configuration
- Verify That You Received Notification of the Scaling Event
- Delete the Notification Configuration

SNS Notifications

Auto Scaling supports sending Amazon SNS notifications when the following events occur.

Event	Description
`autoscaling:EC2_INSTANCE_LAUNCH`	Successful instance launch
`autoscaling:EC2_INSTANCE_LAUNCH_ERROR`	Failed instance launch
`autoscaling:EC2_INSTANCE_TERMINATE`	Successful instance termination
`autoscaling:EC2_INSTANCE_TERMINATE_ERR`	Failed instance termination

The message includes the following information:

- **Event** — The event.
- **AccountId** — The AWS account ID.
- **AutoScalingGroupName** — The name of the Auto Scaling group.
- **AutoScalingGroupARN** — The ARN of the Auto Scaling group.
- **EC2InstanceId** — The ID of the EC2 instance.

For example:

```
1 Service: AWS Auto Scaling
2 Time: 2016-09-30T19:00:36.414Z
3 RequestId: 4e6156f4-a9e2-4bda-a7fd-33f2ae528958
4 Event: autoscaling:EC2_INSTANCE_LAUNCH
```

```
 5 AccountId: 123456789012
 6 AutoScalingGroupName: my-asg
 7 AutoScalingGroupARN: arn:aws:autoscaling:us-west-2:123456789012:autoScalingGroup...
 8 ActivityId: 4e6156f4-a9e2-4bda-a7fd-33f2ae528958
 9 Description: Launching a new EC2 instance: i-0598c7d356eba48d7
10 Cause: At 2016-09-30T18:59:38Z a user request update of AutoScalingGroup constraints to ...
11 StartTime: 2016-09-30T19:00:04.445Z
12 EndTime: 2016-09-30T19:00:36.414Z
13 StatusCode: InProgress
14 StatusMessage:
15 Progress: 50
16 EC2InstanceId: i-0598c7d356eba48d7
17 Details: {"Subnet ID":"subnet-c9663da0","Availability Zone":"us-west-2b"}
```

Configure Amazon SNS

To use Amazon SNS to send email notifications, you must first create a *topic* and then subscribe your email addresses to the topic.

Create an Amazon SNS Topic

An SNS topic is a logical access point, a communication channel your Auto Scaling group uses to send the notifications. You create a topic by specifying a name for your topic.

For more information, see Create a Topic in the *Amazon Simple Notification Service Developer Guide*.

Subscribe to the Amazon SNS Topic

To receive the notifications that your Auto Scaling group sends to the topic, you must subscribe an endpoint to the topic. In this procedure, for **Endpoint**, specify the email address where you want to receive the notifications from Auto Scaling.

For more information, see Subscribe to a Topic in the *Amazon Simple Notification Service Developer Guide*.

Confirm Your Amazon SNS Subscription

Amazon SNS sends a confirmation email to the email address you specified in the previous step.

Make sure you open the email from AWS Notifications and choose the link to confirm the subscription before you continue with the next step.

You will receive an acknowledgement message from AWS. Amazon SNS is now configured to receive notifications and send the notification as an email to the email address that you specified.

Configure Your Auto Scaling Group to Send Notifications

You can configure your Auto Scaling group to send notifications to Amazon SNS when a scaling event, such as launching instances or terminating instances, takes place. Amazon SNS sends a notification with information about the instances to the email address that you specified.

To configure Amazon SNS notifications for your Auto Scaling group using the console

1. Open the Amazon EC2 console at https://console.aws.amazon.com/ec2/.

2. On the navigation pane, under **Auto Scaling**, choose **Auto Scaling Groups**.

3. Select your Auto Scaling group.

4. On the **Notifications** tab, choose **Create notification**.

5. On the **Create notifications** pane, do the following:

   1. For **Send a notification to:**, select your SNS topic.

   2. For **Whenever instances**, select the events to send the notifications for.

   3. Choose **Save**.

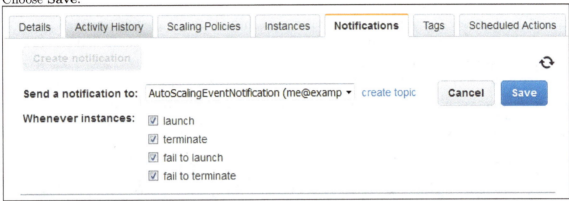

To configure Amazon SNS notifications for your Auto Scaling group using the AWS CLI

Use the following put-notification-configuration command:

```
1 aws autoscaling put-notification-configuration --auto-scaling-group-name my-asg --topic-arn arn
    --notification-types "autoscaling:EC2_INSTANCE_LAUNCH" "autoscaling:EC2_INSTANCE_TERMINATE"
```

Test the Notification Configuration

To generate a notification for a launch event, update the Auto Scaling group by increasing the desired capacity of the Auto Scaling group by 1. Auto Scaling launches the EC2 instance, and you'll receive an email notification within a few minutes.

To change the desired capacity using the console

1. Open the Amazon EC2 console at https://console.aws.amazon.com/ec2/.

2. On the navigation pane, under **Auto Scaling**, choose **Auto Scaling Groups**.

3. Select your Auto Scaling group.

4. On the **Details** tab, choose **Edit**.

5. For **Desired**, increase the current value by 1. Note that if this value exceeds **Max**, you must also increase the value of **Max** by 1.

6. Choose **Save**.

7. After a few minutes, you'll receive a notification email for the launch event. If you do not need the additional instance that you launched for this test, you can decrease **Desired** by 1. After a few minutes, you'll receive a notification email for the terminate event.

To change the desired capacity using the AWS CLI

Use the following set-desired-capacity command:

```
1 aws autoscaling set-desired-capacity --auto-scaling-group-name my-asg --desired-capacity 2
```

Verify That You Received Notification of the Scaling Event

Check your email for a message from Amazon SNS and open the email. After you receive notification of a scaling event for your Auto Scaling group, you can confirm the scaling event by looking at the description of your Auto Scaling group. You'll need information from the notification email, such as the ID of the instance that was launched or terminated.

To verify that your Auto Scaling group has launched new instance using the console

1. Select your Auto Scaling group.

2. On the **Activity History** tab, the **Status** column shows the current status of your instance. For example, if the notification indicates that an instance has launched, use the refresh button to verify that the status of the launch activity is **Successful**.

3. On the **Instances** tab, you can view the current **Lifecycle** state of the instance whose ID you received in the notification email. After a new instance starts, its lifecycle state changes to `InService`.

To verify that your Auto Scaling group has launched new instance using the AWS CLI
Use the following describe-auto-scaling-groups command to confirm that the size of your Auto Scaling group has changed:

```
1 aws autoscaling describe-auto-scaling-groups --auto-scaling-group-name my-asg
```

The following example output shows that the group has two instances. Check for the instance whose ID you received in the notification email.

```
1  {
2      "AutoScalingGroups": [
3          {
4              "AutoScalingGroupARN": "arn",
5              "HealthCheckGracePeriod": 0,
6              "SuspendedProcesses": [],
7              "DesiredCapacity": 2,
8              "Tags": [],
9              "EnabledMetrics": [],
10             "LoadBalancerNames": [],
11             "AutoScalingGroupName": "my-asg",
12             "DefaultCooldown": 300,
13             "MinSize": 1,
14             "Instances": [
15                 {
16                     "InstanceId": "i-d95eb0d4",
17                     "AvailabilityZone": "us-west-2b",
18                     "HealthStatus": "Healthy",
19                     "LifecycleState": "InService",
20                     "LaunchConfigurationName": "my-lc"
21                 },
22                 {
23                     "InstanceId": "i-13d7dc1f",
24                     "AvailabilityZone": "us-west-2a",
25                     "HealthStatus": "Healthy",
26                     "LifecycleState": "InService",
27                     "LaunchConfigurationName": "my-lc"
28                 }
29             ],
30             "MaxSize": 5,
31             "VPCZoneIdentifier": null,
```

```
32        "TerminationPolicies": [
33            "Default"
34        ],
35        "LaunchConfigurationName": "my-lc",
36        "CreatedTime": "2015-03-01T16:12:35.608Z",
37        "AvailabilityZones": [
38            "us-west-2b",
39            "us-west-2a"
40        ],
41        "HealthCheckType": "EC2"
42    }
43  ]
44 }
```

Delete the Notification Configuration

You can delete your Auto Scaling notification configuration at any time.

To delete Auto Scaling notification configuration using the console

1. Open the Amazon EC2 console at https://console.aws.amazon.com/ec2/.

2. On the navigation pane, under **Auto Scaling**, choose **Auto Scaling Groups**.

3. Select your Auto Scaling group.

4. On the **Notifications** tab, choose **Delete** next to the notification.

To delete Auto Scaling notification configuration using the AWS CLI
Use the following delete-notification-configuration command:

```
1 aws autoscaling delete-notification-configuration --auto-scaling-group-name my-asg --topic-arn
    arn:aws:sns:us-west-2:123456789012:my-sns-topic
```

For information about deleting the Amazon SNS topic associated with your Auto Scaling group, and also deleting all the subscriptions to that topic, see Clean Up in the *Amazon Simple Notification Service Developer Guide.*

Logging Amazon EC2 Auto Scaling API Calls By Using AWS Cloud-Trail

Amazon EC2 Auto Scaling is integrated with CloudTrail, a service that captures API calls made by or on behalf of Auto Scaling in your AWS account and delivers the log files to an Amazon S3 bucket that you specify. CloudTrail captures API calls from the Auto Scaling console or from the Auto Scaling API. Using the information collected by CloudTrail, you can determine what request was made to Auto Scaling, the source IP address from which the request was made, who made the request, when it was made, and so on. For more information about CloudTrail, including how to configure and enable it, see the http://docs.aws.amazon.com/awscloudtrail/latest/userguide/.

Auto Scaling Information in CloudTrail

When CloudTrail logging is enabled in your AWS account, API calls made to Auto Scaling actions are tracked in log files. Auto Scaling records are written together with other AWS service records in a log file. CloudTrail determines when to create and write to a new file based on a time period and file size.

All of the Auto Scaling actions are logged and are documented in the Amazon EC2 Auto Scaling API Reference. For example, calls to the **CreateLaunchConfiguration**, **DescribeAutoScalingGroup**, and **UpdateAutoScalingGroup** actions generate entries in the CloudTrail log files.

Every log entry contains information about who generated the request. The user identity information in the log helps you determine whether the request was made with account or IAM user credentials, with temporary security credentials for a role or federated user, or by another AWS service. For more information, see **userIdentity** in the CloudTrail Event Reference section in the *AWS CloudTrail User Guide*.

You can store your log files in your bucket for as long as you want, but you can also define Amazon S3 lifecycle rules to archive or delete log files automatically. By default, your log files are encrypted by using Amazon S3 server-side encryption (SSE).

You can choose to have CloudTrail publish Amazon SNS notifications when new log files are delivered if you want to take quick action upon log file delivery. For more information, see Configuring Amazon SNS Notifications in the *AWS CloudTrail User Guide*.

You can also aggregate Auto Scaling log files from multiple AWS regions and multiple AWS accounts into a single Amazon S3 bucket. For more information, see Aggregating CloudTrail Log Files to a Single Amazon S3 Bucket in the *AWS CloudTrail User Guide*.

Understanding Auto Scaling Log File Entries

CloudTrail log files can contain one or more log entries where each entry is made up of multiple JSON-formatted events. A log entry represents a single request from any source and includes information about the requested action, any parameters, the date and time of the action, and so on. The log entries are not guaranteed to be in any particular order. That is, they are not an ordered stack trace of the public API calls.

The following example shows a CloudTrail log entry that demonstrates the CreateLaunchConfiguration action.

```
1  {
2      "Records": [
3      {
4          "eventVersion": "1.01",
5          "userIdentity": {
6              "type": "IAMUser",
7              "principalId": "EX_PRINCIPAL_ID",
8              "arn": "arn:aws:iam::123456789012:user/iamUser1",
9              "accountId": "123456789012",
```

```
10          "accessKeyId": "EXAMPLE_KEY_ID",
11          "userName": "iamUser1"
12          },
13      "eventTime": "2014-06-24T16:53:14Z",
14      "eventSource": "autoscaling.amazonaws.com",
15      "eventName": "CreateLaunchConfiguration",
16      "awsRegion": "us-west-2",
17      "sourceIPAddress": "192.0.2.0",
18      "userAgent": "Amazon CLI/AutoScaling 1.0.61.3 API 2011-01-01",
19      "requestParameters": {
20          "imageId": "ami-2f726546",
21          "instanceType": "m1.small",
22          "launchConfigurationName": "launch_configuration_1"
23          },
24      "responseElements": null,
25      "requestID": "07a1becf-fbc0-11e3-bfd8-a5209058e7bb",
26      "eventID": "ad30abf7-57db-4a6d-93fa-13deb1fd4cff"
27      },
28      ...additional entries
29  ]
30 }
```

The following example shows a CloudTrail log entry that demonstrates the DescribeAutoScalingGroups action.

```
1 {
2      "Records": [
3      {
4      "eventVersion": "1.01",
5      "userIdentity": {
6          "type": "IAMUser",
7          "principalId": "EX_PRINCIPAL_ID",
8          "arn": "arn:aws:iam::123456789012:user/iamUser1",
9          "accountId": "123456789012",
10          "accessKeyId": "EXAMPLE_KEY_ID",
11          "userName": "iamUser1"
12          },
13      "eventTime": "2014-06-23T23:20:56Z",
14      "eventSource": "autoscaling.amazonaws.com",
15      "eventName": "DescribeAutoScalingGroups",
16      "awsRegion": "us-west-2",
17      "sourceIPAddress": "192.0.2.0",
18      "userAgent": "Amazon CLI/AutoScaling 1.0.61.3 API 2011-01-01",
19      "requestParameters": {
20          "maxRecords": 20
21          },
22      "responseElements": null,
23      "requestID": "0737e2ea-fb2d-11e3-bfd8-a5209058e7bb",
24      "eventID": "0353fb04-281e-47d9-93bb-588bf2256538"
25      },
26      ...additional entries
27  ]
28 }
```

The following example shows a CloudTrail log entry that demonstrates the UpdateAutoScalingGroups action.

```
1 {
```

```
 2      "Records": [
 3      {
 4          "eventVersion": "1.01",
 5          "userIdentity": {
 6              "type": "IAMUser",
 7              "principalId": "EX_PRINCIPAL_ID",
 8              "arn": "arn:aws:iam::123456789012:user/iamUser1",
 9              "accountId": "123456789012",
10              "accessKeyId": "EXAMPLE_KEY_ID",
11              "userName": "iamUser1"
12              },
13          "eventTime": "2014-06-24T16:54:46Z",
14          "eventSource": "autoscaling.amazonaws.com",
15          "eventName": "UpdateAutoScalingGroup",
16          "awsRegion": "us-west-2",
17          "sourceIPAddress": "192.0.2.0",
18          "userAgent": "Amazon CLI/AutoScaling 1.0.61.3 API 2011-01-01",
19          "requestParameters": {
20              "maxSize": 8,
21              "minSize": 1,
22              "autoScalingGroupName": "asg1"
23              },
24          "responseElements": null,
25          "requestID": "3ed07c03-fbc0-11e3-bfd8-a5209058e7bb",
26          "eventID": "b52ca0aa-5199-4873-a546-55f7c896a4ce"
27          },
28          ...additional entries
29      ]
30
31 }
```

Controlling Access to Your Amazon EC2 Auto Scaling Resources

Amazon EC2 Auto Scaling integrates with AWS Identity and Access Management (IAM), a service that enables you to do the following:

- Create users and groups under your organization's AWS account
- Assign unique security credentials to each user under your AWS account
- Control each user's permissions to perform tasks using AWS resources
- Allow the users in another AWS account to share your AWS resources
- Create roles for your AWS account and define the users or services that can assume them
- Use existing identities for your enterprise to grant permissions to perform tasks using AWS resources

For example, you can create an IAM policy that grants the Managers group permission to use only the `DescribeAutoScalingGroups`, `DescribeLaunchConfigurations`, `DescribeScalingActivities`, and `DescribePolicies` API operations. Users in the Managers group could then use those operations with any Auto Scaling groups and launch configurations.

You can also create IAM policies that restrict access to a particular Auto Scaling group or launch configuration.

For more information, see Identity and Access Management (IAM) or the IAM User Guide.

Topics

- Amazon EC2 Auto Scaling Actions
- Amazon EC2 Auto Scaling Resources
- Amazon EC2 Auto Scaling Condition Keys
- Supported Resource-Level Permissions
- Predefined AWS Managed Policies
- Customer Managed Policies
- Service-Linked Roles for Amazon EC2 Auto Scaling
- Launch Auto Scaling Instances with an IAM Role

Amazon EC2 Auto Scaling Actions

You can specify any and all Amazon EC2 Auto Scaling actions in an IAM policy. Use the following prefix with the name of the action: `autoscaling:`. For example:

```
1  "Action": "autoscaling:CreateAutoScalingGroup"
```

To specify multiple actions in a single statement, enclose them in square brackets and separate them with commas, as follows:

```
1  "Action": [
2      "autoscaling:CreateAutoScalingGroup",
3      "autoscaling:UpdateAutoScalingGroup"
4  ]
```

You can also use wildcards. For example, use `autoscaling:*` to specify all Amazon EC2 Auto Scaling actions.

```
1  "Action": "autoscaling:*"
```

Use `Describe:*` to specify all actions whose names start with `Describe`.

```
1  "Action": "autoscaling:Describe*"
```

For more information, see Amazon EC2 Auto Scaling Actions in the *Amazon EC2 Auto Scaling API Reference.*

Required Permissions

When calling the following actions, you must grant IAM users permission to call the action itself, plus additional actions from Amazon EC2 or IAM.

`CreateLaunchConfiguration`

- `autoscaling:CreateLaunchConfiguration`
- `ec2:DescribeImages`
- `ec2:DescribeInstances`
- `ec2:DescribeInstanceAttribute`
- `ec2:DescribeKeyPairs`
- `ec2:DescribeSecurityGroups`
- `ec2:DescribeSpotInstanceRequests`
- `ec2:DescribeVpcClassicLink`

`CreateAutoScalingGroup`

- `autoscaling:CreateAutoScalingGroup`
- `iam:CreateServiceLinkedRole`

Amazon EC2 Auto Scaling Resources

For actions that support resource-level permissions, you can control the Auto Scaling group or launch configuration that users are allowed to access.

To specify an Auto Scaling group, you must specify its Amazon Resource Name (ARN) as follows:

```
1  "Resource": "arn:aws:autoscaling:region:123456789012:autoScalingGroup:uuid:autoScalingGroupName/
       asg-name"
```

To specify an Auto Scaling group with `CreateAutoScalingGroup`, you must replace the UUID with * as follows:

```
1  "Resource": "arn:aws:autoscaling:region:123456789012:autoScalingGroup:*:autoScalingGroupName/asg
       -name"
```

To specify a launch configuration, you must specify its ARN as follows:

```
1  "Resource": "arn:aws:autoscaling:region:123456789012:launchConfiguration:uuid:
       launchConfigurationName/lc-name"
```

To specify a launch configuration with `CreateLaunchConfiguration`, you must replace the UUID with * as follows:

```
1  "Resource": "arn:aws:autoscaling:region:123456789012:launchConfiguration:*:
       launchConfigurationName/lc-name"
```

The following Amazon EC2 Auto Scaling actions do not support resource-level permissions:

- `DescribeAccountLimits`
- `DescribeAdjustmentTypes`
- `DescribeAutoScalingGroups`
- `DescribeAutoScalingInstances`
- `DescribeAutoScalingNotificationTypes`
- `DescribeLaunchConfigurations`
- `DescribeLifecycleHooks`
- `DescribeLifecycleHookTypes`
- `DescribeLoadBalancers`
- `DescribeLoadBalancerTargetGroups`

- `DescribeMetricCollectionTypes`
- `DescribeNotificationConfigurations`
- `DescribePolicies`
- `DescribeScalingActivities`
- `DescribeScalingProcessTypes`
- `DescribeScheduledActions`
- `DescribeTags`
- `DescribeTerminationPolicyTypes`

For actions that don't support resource-level permissions, you must use "*" as the resource.

```
1 "Resource": "*"
```

Amazon EC2 Auto Scaling Condition Keys

When you create a policy, you can specify the conditions that control when the policy is in effect. Each condition contains one or more key-value pairs. There are global condition keys and service-specific condition keys.

The following condition keys are specific to Amazon EC2 Auto Scaling:

- `autoscaling:ImageId`
- `autoscaling:InstanceType`
- `autoscaling:LaunchConfigurationName`
- `autoscaling:LaunchTemplateVersionSpecified`
- `autoscaling:LoadBalancerNames`
- `autoscaling:MaxSize`
- `autoscaling:MinSize`
- `autoscaling:ResourceTag/key`
- `autoscaling:SpotPrice`
- `autoscaling:TargetGroupARNs`
- `autoscaling:VPCZoneIdentifiers`

For more information about global condition keys, see AWS Global Condition Context Keys in the *IAM User Guide*.

Supported Resource-Level Permissions

The following table describes the Amazon EC2 Auto Scaling API actions that support resource-level permissions, as well as the supported condition keys and resources for each action.

API Action	Condition Keys	Resource ARN
AttachInstances	autoscaling:ResourceTag/key	Auto Scaling group
AttachLoadBalancers	`autoscaling:` `LoadBalancerNames,` autoscaling:ResourceTag/ key	Auto Scaling group
AttachLoadBalancerTarget-Groups	autoscaling:ResourceTag /key, `autoscaling:` `TargetGroupARNs`	Auto Scaling group
CompleteLifecycleAction	autoscaling:ResourceTag/key	Auto Scaling group

API Action	Condition Keys	Resource ARN
CreateAutoScalingGroup	`autoscaling:` `LaunchConfigurationName` `,` `autoscaling:` `LaunchTemplateVersionSpeci` `,` `autoscaling:` `LoadBalancerNames,` `autoscaling:MaxSize` `,` `autoscaling:MinSize,` `autoscaling:ResourceTag` `/key,` `autoscaling` `:TargetGroupARNs` `,` `autoscaling:` `VPCZoneIdentifiers,` `aws:RequestTag/key,` `aws:` `TagKeys`	Auto Scaling group (replace UUID with *)
CreateLaunchConfiguration	`autoscaling:ImageId,` `autoscaling:InstanceType,` `autoscaling:SpotPrice`	Launch configuration (replace UUID with *)
CreateOrUpdateTags	`autoscaling:ResourceTag` `/key,` `aws:RequestTag/key,` `aws:TagKeys`	Auto Scaling group
DeleteAutoScalingGroup	autoscaling:ResourceTag/key	Auto Scaling group
DeleteLaunchConfiguration		Launch configuration
DeleteLifecycleHook	autoscaling:ResourceTag/key	Auto Scaling group
DeleteNotificationConfiguration	autoscaling:ResourceTag/key	Auto Scaling group
DeletePolicy	autoscaling:ResourceTag/key	Auto Scaling group
DeleteScheduledAction	autoscaling:ResourceTag/key	Auto Scaling group
DeleteTags	`autoscaling:ResourceTag` `/key,` `aws:RequestTag/key,` `aws:TagKeys`	Auto Scaling group
DetachInstances	autoscaling:ResourceTag/key	Auto Scaling group
DetachLoadBalancers	`autoscaling:` `LoadBalancerNames,` `autoscaling:ResourceTag/` `key`	Auto Scaling group
DetachLoadBalancerTargetGroups	`autoscaling:ResourceTag` `/key,` `autoscaling:` `TargetGroupARNs`	Auto Scaling group
DisableMetricsCollection	autoscaling:ResourceTag/key	Auto Scaling group
EnableMetricsCollection	autoscaling:ResourceTag/key	Auto Scaling group
EnterStandby	autoscaling:ResourceTag/key	Auto Scaling group
ExecutePolicy	autoscaling:ResourceTag/key	Auto Scaling group
ExitStandby	autoscaling:ResourceTag/key	Auto Scaling group
PutLifecycleHook	autoscaling:ResourceTag/key	Auto Scaling group
PutNotificationConfiguration	autoscaling:ResourceTag/key	Auto Scaling group
PutScalingPolicy	autoscaling:ResourceTag/key	Auto Scaling group
PutScheduledUpdateGroupAction	`autoscaling:MaxSize` `,` `autoscaling:MinSize,` `autoscaling:ResourceTag/` `key`	Auto Scaling group
RecordLifecycleActionHeartbeat	autoscaling:ResourceTag/key	Auto Scaling group

API Action	Condition Keys	Resource ARN
ResumeProcesses	autoscaling:ResourceTag/key	Auto Scaling group
SetDesiredCapacity	autoscaling:ResourceTag/key	Auto Scaling group
SetInstanceHealth	autoscaling:ResourceTag/key	Auto Scaling group
SetInstanceProtection	autoscaling:ResourceTag/key	Auto Scaling group
SuspendProcesses	autoscaling:ResourceTag/key	Auto Scaling group
TerminateInstanceInAutoScalingGroup	autoscaling:ResourceTag/key	Auto Scaling group
UpdateAutoScalingGroup	`autoscaling:LaunchConfigurationName`, `autoscaling:LaunchTemplateVersionSpeci`, `autoscaling:MaxSize`, `autoscaling:MinSize`, `autoscaling:ResourceTag/key`, `autoscaling:VPCZoneIdentifiers`	Auto Scaling group

Predefined AWS Managed Policies

The managed policies created by AWS grant the required permissions for common use cases. You can attach these policies to your IAM users, based on the access that they need. Each policy grants access to all or some of the API actions for Amazon EC2 Auto Scaling, plus additional API actions for Amazon EC2, CloudWatch, Elastic Load Balancing, IAM, and Amazon SNS.

The following are the AWS managed policies for Amazon EC2 Auto Scaling:

- **AutoScalingConsoleFullAccess** — Grants full access to Amazon EC2 Auto Scaling using the AWS Management Console.
- **AutoScalingConsoleReadOnlyAccess** — Grants read-only access to Amazon EC2 Auto Scaling using the AWS Management Console.
- **AutoScalingFullAccess** — Grants full access to Amazon EC2 Auto Scaling.
- **AutoScalingReadOnlyAccess** — Grants read-only access to Amazon EC2 Auto Scaling.

Customer Managed Policies

You can create custom IAM policies that grant your IAM users permissions to perform specific actions on specific resources. The following are example policies for Amazon EC2 Auto Scaling.

Example: Require a Launch Template

When you create or update an Auto Scaling group, you can specify a launch template, a launch configuration, or an EC2 instance. When you specify a launch template, you can configure the Auto Scaling group to use a specific launch template version, the latest version, or the default version when launching instances.

The `autoscaling:LaunchTemplateVersionSpecified` condition key is a Boolean value that is set as follows:

- `null` - If no launch template is specified
- `true` - If a specific launch template version is used
- `false` - If either the latest or default launch template version is used

The following policy grants users permission to create or update an Auto Scaling group using a specific launch template version, and access the Amazon EC2 resources specified in the launch template.

149

```
1  {
2      "Version": "2012-10-17",
3      "Statement": [
4          {
5              "Effect": "Allow",
6              "Action": [
7                  "autoscaling:CreateAutoScalingGroup",
8                  "autoscaling:UpdateAutoScalingGroup"
9              ],
10             "Resource": "*",
11             "Condition": {
12                 "Bool": {
13                     "autoscaling:LaunchTemplateVersionSpecified": "true"
14                 }
15             }
16         },
17         {
18             "Effect": "Allow",
19             "Action": [
20                 "ec2:*"
21             ],
22             "Resource": "*"
23         }
24     ]
25 }
```

Example: Create and Manage Launch Configurations

The following policy grants users permission to use all Amazon EC2 Auto Scaling actions that include the string LaunchConfiguration in their names. Alternatively, you can list each action explicitly instead of using wildcards. However, the policy would not automatically apply to any new Amazon EC2 Auto Scaling actions with LaunchConfiguration in their names.

```
1  {
2      "Version": "2012-10-17",
3      "Statement": [{
4          "Effect": "Allow",
5          "Action": "autoscaling:*LaunchConfiguration*",
6          "Resource": "*"
7      }]
8  }
```

The following policy grants users permission to create a launch configuration if the instance type is t2.micro and the name of the launch configuration starts with **t2micro-**, and specify a launch configuration for an Auto Scaling group only if its name starts with **t2micro-**.

```
1  {
2      "Version": "2012-10-17",
3      "Statement": [
4      {
5          "Effect": "Allow",
6          "Action": "autoscaling:CreateLaunchConfiguration",
7          "Resource": [
8              "arn:aws:autoscaling:us-east-2:123456789012:launchConfiguration:*:
                   launchConfigurationName/t2micro-*"
```

```
 9          ],
10          "Condition": {
11              "StringEquals": { "autoscaling:InstanceType": "t2.micro" }
12          }
13      },
14      {
15          "Effect": "Allow",
16          "Action": [
17              "autoscaling:CreateAutoScalingGroup",
18              "autoscaling:UpdateAutoScalingGroup"
19          ],
20          "Resource": "*",
21          "Condition": {
22              "StringLikeIfExists": { "autoscaling:LaunchConfigurationName": "t2micro-*" }
23          }
24      }]
25 }
```

Example: Create and Manage Auto Scaling Groups and Scaling Policies

The following policy grants users permission to use all Amazon EC2 Auto Scaling actions that include the string Scaling in their names.

```
1 {
2      "Version": "2012-10-17",
3      "Statement": [{
4          "Effect": "Allow",
5          "Action": ["autoscaling:*Scaling*"],
6          "Resource": "*"
7      }]
8 }
```

The following policy grants users permission to use all Amazon EC2 Auto Scaling actions that include the string Scaling in their names, as long as the Auto Scaling group has the tag **purpose=webserver**. Because the Describe actions do not support resource-level permissions, you must specify them in a separate statement without conditions.

```
 1 {
 2      "Version": "2012-10-17",
 3      "Statement": [
 4      {
 5          "Effect": "Allow",
 6          "Action": ["autoscaling:*Scaling*"],
 7          "Resource": "*",
 8          "Condition": {
 9              "StringEquals": { "autoscaling:ResourceTag/purpose": "webserver" }
10          }
11      },
12      {
13          "Effect": "Allow",
14          "Action": "autoscaling:Describe*Scaling*",
15          "Resource": "*"
16      }]
17 }
```

The following policy grants users permission to use all Amazon EC2 Auto Scaling actions that include the string `Scaling` in their names, as long as they don't specify a minimum size less than 1 or a maximum size greater than 10. Because the `Describe` actions do not support resource-level permissions, you must specify them in a separate statement without conditions.

```
1  {
2      "Version": "2012-10-17",
3      "Statement": [
4      {
5          "Effect": "Allow",
6          "Action": ["autoscaling:*Scaling*"],
7          "Resource": "*",
8          "Condition": {
9              "NumericGreaterThanEqualsIfExists": { "autoscaling:MinSize": 1 },
10             "NumericLessThanEqualsIfExists": { "autoscaling:MaxSize": 10 }
11         }
12     },
13     {
14         "Effect": "Allow",
15         "Action": "autoscaling:Describe*Scaling*",
16         "Resource": "*"
17     }]
18 }
```

Example: Control Access Using Tags

To grant users permission to create or tag an Auto Scaling group only if they specify specific tags, use the `aws:RequestTag` condition key. To allow only specific tag keys, use the `aws:TagKeys` condition key with the `ForAnyValue` modifier.

The following policy requires users to tag any Auto Scaling groups with the tags **purpose=webserver** and **cost-center=cc123**, and allows only the **purpose** and ****cost-center **** tags (no other tags can be specified).

```
1  {
2      "Version": "2012-10-17",
3      "Statement": [{
4          "Effect": "Allow",
5          "Action": [
6              "autoscaling:CreateAutoScalingGroup",
7              "autoscaling:CreateOrUpdateTags"
8          ],
9          "Resource": "*",
10         "Condition": {
11             "StringEquals": {
12                 "aws:RequestTag/purpose": "webserver",
13                 "aws:RequestTag/cost-center": "cc123"
14             },
15             "ForAllValues:StringEquals": { "aws:TagKeys": ["purpose", "cost-center"] }
16         }
17     }]
18 }
```

The following policy requires users to specify a tag with the key **environment** in the request.

```
1  {
2      "Version": "2012-10-17",
```

```
3    "Statement": [{
4       "Effect": "Allow",
5       "Action": [
6          "autoscaling:CreateAutoScalingGroup",
7          "autoscaling:CreateOrUpdateTags"
8       ],
9       "Resource": "*",
10      "Condition": {
11         "StringLike": { "aws:RequestTag/environment": "*" }
12      }
13   }]
14 }
```

The following policy requires users to specify at least one tag in the request, and allows only the **cost-center** and **owner** keys.

```
1  {
2     "Version": "2012-10-17",
3     "Statement": [{
4        "Effect": "Allow",
5        "Action": [
6           "autoscaling:CreateAutoScalingGroup",
7           "autoscaling:CreateOrUpdateTags"
8        ],
9        "Resource": "*",
10       "Condition": {
11          "ForAnyValue:StringEquals": { "aws:TagKeys": ["cost-center", "owner"] }
12       }
13    }]
14 }
```

The following policy grants users access to Auto Scaling groups with the tag **allowed=true** and allows them to apply only the tag **environment=test**. Because launch configurations do not support tags and `Describe` actions do not support resource-level permissions, you must specify them in a separate statement without conditions.

```
1  {
2     "Version": "2012-10-17",
3     "Statement": [{
4        "Effect": "Allow",
5        "Action": "autoscaling:*Scaling*",
6        "Resource": "*",
7        "Condition": {
8           "StringEquals": { "autoscaling:ResourceTag/allowed": "true" },
9           "StringEqualsIfExists": { "aws:RequestTag/environment": "test" },
10          "ForAllValues:StringEquals": { "aws:TagKeys": "environment" }
11       }
12    },
13    {
14       "Effect": "Allow",
15       "Action": [
16          "autoscaling:*LaunchConfiguration*",
17          "autoscaling:Describe*"
18       ],
19       "Resource": "*"
20    }]
```

```
21 }
```

Example: Change the Capacity of Auto Scaling Groups

The following policy grants users permission to use the `SetDesiredCapacity` action to change the capacity of any Auto Scaling group.

```
1 {
2     "Version": "2012-10-17",
3     "Statement": [{
4         "Effect": "Allow",
5         "Action": "autoscaling:SetDesiredCapacity",
6         "Resource": "*"
7     }]
8 }
```

The following policy grants users permission to use the `SetDesiredCapacity` action to change the capacity of the specified Auto Scaling groups. Note that including the UUID ensures that access is granted to the specific Auto Scaling group. If you were to delete an Auto Scaling group and create a new one with the same name, the UUID for the new group would be different than the UUID for the original group.

```
1 {
2     "Version": "2012-10-17",
3     "Statement": [{
4         "Effect": "Allow",
5         "Action": "autoscaling:SetDesiredCapacity",
6         "Resource": [
7             "arn:aws:autoscaling:us-east-2:123456789012:autoScalingGroup:7fe02b8e-7442-4c9e-8c8e
                -85fa99e9b5d9:autoScalingGroupName/group-1",
8             "arn:aws:autoscaling:us-east-2:123456789012:autoScalingGroup:9d8e8ea4-22e1-44c7-a14d
                -520f8518c2b9:autoScalingGroupName/group-2",
9             "arn:aws:autoscaling:us-east-2:123456789012:autoScalingGroup:60d6b363-ae8b-467c-947f-
                f1d308935521:autoScalingGroupName/group-3"
10        ]
11    }]
12 }
```

The following policy grants users permission to use the `SetDesiredCapacity` action to change the capacity of any Auto Scaling group whose name begins with **group-**.

```
1 {
2     "Version": "2012-10-17",
3     "Statement": [{
4         "Effect": "Allow",
5         "Action": "autoscaling:SetDesiredCapacity",
6         "Resource": [
7             "arn:aws:autoscaling:us-east-2:123456789012:autoScalingGroup:*:autoScalingGroupName/
                group-*"
8         ]
9     }]
10 }
```

Service-Linked Roles for Amazon EC2 Auto Scaling

Amazon EC2 Auto Scaling uses service-linked roles for the permissions that it requires to call other AWS services on your behalf. For more information, see Using Service-Linked Roles in the *IAM User Guide*.

Permissions Granted by AWSServiceRoleForAutoScaling

By default, Amazon EC2 Auto Scaling uses the **AWSServiceRoleForAutoScaling** service-linked role to make the following calls on your behalf. Alternatively, you can create a service-linked role for Amazon EC2 Auto Scaling to use to make the following calls on your behalf.

- `ec2:AttachClassicLinkVpc`
- `ec2:CancelSpotInstanceRequests`
- `ec2:CreateTags`
- `ec2:DeleteTags`
- `ec2:Describe*`
- `ec2:DetachClassicLinkVpc`
- `ec2:ModifyInstanceAttribute`
- `ec2:RequestSpotInstances`
- `ec2:RunInstances`
- `ec2:TerminateInstances`
- `elasticloadbalancing:Register*`
- `elasticloadbalancing:Deregister*`
- `elasticloadbalancing:Describe*`
- `cloudwatch:DeleteAlarms`
- `cloudwatch:DescribeAlarms`
- `cloudwatch:PutMetricAlarm`
- `sns:Publish`

This role trusts the `autoscaling.amazonaws.com` service to assume it.

If you specify encrypted EBS volumes for your Auto Scaling instances and you use customer managed CMKs for encryption, you must grant the appropriate service-linked role access to the CMKs so that the Auto Scaling group can launch instances on your behalf. The principal is the Amazon Resource Name (ARN) of the service-linked role. When launching On-Demand instances, use a service-linked role for Amazon EC2 Auto Scaling. When launching Spot Instances, use the **AWSServiceRoleForEC2Spot** role when using a launch configuration and a service-linked role for Amazon EC2 Auto Scaling when using a launch template. For more information, see Using Key Policies in AWS KMS in the *AWS Key Management Service Developer Guide*. If the CMKs are in a different account than the service-linked role, you must also create a grant. For more information, see Using Grants in the *AWS Key Management Service Developer Guide*.

You must configure permissions to allow an IAM entity (such as a user, group, or role) to create, edit, or delete a service-linked role. For more information, see Service-Linked Role Permissions in the *IAM User Guide*.

Create the Service-Linked Role

Amazon EC2 Auto Scaling creates the **AWSServiceRoleForAutoScaling** service-linked role for you the first time that you create an Auto Scaling group but do not specify a service-linked role.

If you created an Auto Scaling group before March 2018, when Amazon EC2 Auto Scaling began supporting service-linked roles, Amazon EC2 Auto Scaling created the **AWSServiceRoleForAutoScaling** role in your AWS account. For more information, see A New Role Appeared in My AWS Account in the *IAM User Guide*.

Alternatively, you can specify a service-linked role that you've created when you create your Auto Scaling group. This enables you to grant different service-linked roles access to different KMS keys. You can also track which

Auto Scaling group made an API call in your CloudTrail logs by noting the service-linked role in use.

Use the following create-service-linked-role command to create a service-linked role for Amazon EC2 Auto Scaling with the name **AWSServiceRoleForAutoScaling**_*suffix*. The suffix helps you identify the purpose of the role.

```
1 aws iam create-service-linked-role --aws-service-name autoscaling.amazonaws.com --custom-suffix
    suffix
```

The output of this command includes the ARN of the service-linked role, which you can use to grant the service-linked role access to your KMS keys.

To create the service-linked role using the AWS Management Console, see Creating a Service-Linked Role in the *IAM User Guide*.

Edit the Service-Linked Role

With the **AWSServiceRoleForAutoScaling** role created by Amazon EC2 Auto Scaling, you can edit its description using IAM. You can edit any service-linked role that you created for use with your Auto Scaling groups. For more information, see Editing a Service-Linked Role in the *IAM User Guide*.

Delete the Service-Linked Role

If you no longer need to use an Auto Scaling group, we recommend that you delete its service-linked role.

You can delete a service-linked role only after first deleting the related AWS resources. If a service-linked role is used with multiple Auto Scaling groups, you must delete all Auto Scaling groups that use the service-linked role before you can delete it. This protects your resources because you can't inadvertently remove permission to access them. For more information, see Deleting Your Auto Scaling Infrastructure.

You can use IAM to delete the default service-linked role or one that you've created. For more information, see Deleting a Service-Linked Role in the *IAM User Guide*.

After you delete the **AWSServiceRoleForAutoScaling** service-linked role, Amazon EC2 Auto Scaling will create the role again when you create an Auto Scaling group but do not specify a different service-linked role.

Launch Auto Scaling Instances with an IAM Role

AWS Identity and Access Management (IAM) roles for EC2 instances make it easier for you to access other AWS services securely from within the EC2 instances. EC2 instances launched with an IAM role automatically have AWS security credentials available.

You can launch your Auto Scaling instances with an IAM role to automatically enable applications running on your instances to securely access other AWS resources. You do this by creating a launch configuration with an EC2 instance profile. An instance profile is a container for an IAM role. First, create an IAM role that has all the permissions required to access the AWS resources, then add your role to the instance profile.

For more information about IAM roles and instance profiles, see IAM Roles in the *IAM User Guide*.

Prerequisites

Create an IAM role for your EC2 instances. The console creates an instance profile with the same name as the IAM role.

To create an IAM role

1. Open the IAM console at https://console.aws.amazon.com/iam/.

2. In the navigation pane, choose **Roles**, **Create new role**.

3. On the **Select role type** page, choose **Select** next to **Amazon EC2**.

4. On the **Attach Policy** page, select an AWS managed policy that grants your instances access to the resources that they need.

5. On the **Set role name and review** page, type a name for the role and choose **Create role**.

Create a Launch Configuration

When you create the launch configuration using the AWS Management Console, on the **Configure Details** page, select the role from **IAM role**. For more information, see Creating a Launch Configuration.

When you create the launch configuration using the create-launch-configuration command from the AWS CLI, specify the name of the instance profile as follows:

```
1 aws autoscaling create-launch-configuration --launch-configuration-name my-lc-with-instance-
     profile \
2 --image-id ami-baba68d3 --instance-type m1.small \
3 --iam-instance-profile my-instance-profile
```

Troubleshooting Amazon EC2 Auto Scaling

Amazon EC2 Auto Scaling provides specific and descriptive errors to help you troubleshoot issues. You can find the error messages in the description of the scaling activities.

Topics

- Retrieving an Error Message
- Troubleshooting Amazon EC2 Auto Scaling: EC2 Instance Launch Failures
- Troubleshooting Amazon EC2 Auto Scaling: AMI Issues
- Troubleshooting Amazon EC2 Auto Scaling: Load Balancer Issues
- Troubleshooting Auto Scaling: Capacity Limits

Retrieving an Error Message

To retrieve an error message from the description of scaling activities, use the describe-scaling-activities command as follows:

```
1 aws autoscaling describe-scaling-activities --auto-scaling-group-name my-asg
```

The following is an example response, where `StatusCode` contains the current status of the activity and `StatusMessage` contains the error message:

```
1  {
2      "Activities": [
3          {
4              "Description": "Launching a new EC2 instance: i-4ba0837f",
5              "AutoScalingGroupName": "my-asg",
6              "ActivityId": "f9f2d65b-f1f2-43e7-b46d-d86756459699",
7              "Details": "{"Availability Zone":"us-west-2c"}",
8              "StartTime": "2013-08-19T20:53:29.930Z",
9              "Progress": 100,
10             "EndTime": "2013-08-19T20:54:02Z",
11             "Cause": "At 2013-08-19T20:53:25Z a user request created an AutoScalingGroup...",
12             "StatusCode": "Failed",
13             "StatusMessage": "The image id 'ami-4edb0327' does not exist. Launching EC2 instance
                   failed."
14         }
15     ]
16 }
```

The following tables list the types of error messages and provide links to the troubleshooting resources that you can use to troubleshoot issues.

EC2 Instance Launch Failures

Issue	Error Message
Auto Scaling group	AutoScalingGroup not found.
Availability Zone	The requested Availability Zone is no longer supported. Please retry your request ......
AWS account	You are not subscribed to this service. Please see http://aws.amazon.com.
Block device mapping	Invalid device name upload. Launching EC2 instance failed.
Block device mapping	Value () for parameter virtualName is invalid...

Issue	Error Message
Block device mapping	EBS block device mappings not supported for instance-store AMIs.
Instance type and Availability Zone	Your requested instance type () is not supported in your requested Availability Zone ()....
Key pair	The key pair does not exist. Launching EC2 instance failed.
Launch configuration	The requested configuration is currently not supported.
Placement group	Placement groups may not be used with instances of type 'm1.large'. Launching EC2 instance failed.
Security group	The security group does not exist. Launching EC2 instance failed.

AMI Issues

Issue	Error Message
AMI ID	The AMI ID does not exist. Launching EC2 instance failed.
AMI ID	AMI is pending, and cannot be run. Launching EC2 instance failed.
AMI ID	Value () for parameter virtualName is invalid.
Architecture mismatch	The requested instance type's architecture (i386) does not match the architecture in the manifest for ami-6622f00f (x86_64). Launching ec2 instance failed.

Load Balancer Issues

Issue	Error Message
Cannot find load balancer	Cannot find Load Balancer . Validating load balancer configuration failed.
Instances in VPC	EC2 instance is not in VPC. Updating load balancer configuration failed.
No active load balancer	There is no ACTIVE Load Balancer named . Updating load balancer configuration failed.
Security token	The security token included in the request is invalid. Validating load balancer configuration failed.

Capacity Limits

Issue	Error Message
Capacity limits	instance(s) are already running. Launching EC2 instance failed.
Insufficient capacity in Availability Zone	We currently do not have sufficient capacity in the Availability Zone you requested ()....

Troubleshooting Amazon EC2 Auto Scaling: EC2 Instance Launch Failures

This page provides information about your EC2 instances that fail to launch, potential causes, and the steps you can take to resolve the issues.

To retrieve an error message, see Retrieving an Error Message.

When your EC2 instances fail to launch, you might get one or more of the following error messages:

Topics

- The security group does not exist. Launching EC2 instance failed.
- The key pair does not exist. Launching EC2 instance failed.
- The requested configuration is currently not supported.
- AutoScalingGroup not found.
- The requested Availability Zone is no longer supported. Please retry your request ......
- Your requested instance type () is not supported in your requested Availability Zone ()....
- You are not subscribed to this service. Please see http://aws.amazon.com.
- Invalid device name upload. Launching EC2 instance failed.
- Value () for parameter virtualName is invalid...
- EBS block device mappings not supported for instance-store AMIs.
- Placement groups may not be used with instances of type 'm1.large'. Launching EC2 instance failed.

The security group does not exist. Launching EC2 instance failed.

- **Cause**: The security group specified in your launch configuration might have been deleted.
- **Solution**:
    1. Use the describe-security-groups command to get the list of the security groups associated with your account.
    2. From the list, select the security groups to use. To create a security group instead, use the create-security-group command.
    3. Create a new launch configuration.
    4. Update your Auto Scaling group with the new launch configuration using the update-auto-scaling-group command.

The key pair does not exist. Launching EC2 instance failed.

- **Cause**: The key pair that was used when launching the instance might have been deleted.
- **Solution**:
    1. Use the describe-key-pairs command to get the list of the key pairs available to you.
    2. From the list, select the key pair to use. To create a key pair instead, use the create-key-pair command.
    3. Create a new launch configuration.
    4. Update your Auto Scaling group with the new launch configuration using the update-auto-scaling-group command.

The requested configuration is currently not supported.

- **Cause**: Some options in your launch configuration might not be currently supported.
- **Solution**:
  1. Create a new launch configuration.
  2. Update your Auto Scaling group with the new launch configuration using the update-auto-scaling-group command.

AutoScalingGroup not found.

- **Cause**: The Auto Scaling group might have been deleted.
- **Solution**: Create a new Auto Scaling group.

The requested Availability Zone is no longer supported. Please retry your request ......

- **Error Message**: The requested Availability Zone is no longer supported. Please retry your request by not specifying an Availability Zone or choosing . Launching EC2 instance failed.
- **Cause**: The Availability Zone associated with your Auto Scaling group might not be currently available.
- **Solution**: Update your Auto Scaling group with the recommendations in the error message.

Your requested instance type () is not supported in your requested Availability Zone ()....

- **Error Message**: Your requested instance type () is not supported in your requested Availability Zone (). Please retry your request by not specifying an Availability Zone or choosing . Launching EC2 instance failed.
- **Cause**: The instance type associated with your launch configuration might not be currently available in the Availability Zones specified in your Auto Scaling group.
- **Solution**: Update your Auto Scaling group with the recommendations in the error message.

You are not subscribed to this service. Please see http://aws/.amazon/.com/.

- **Cause**: Your AWS account might have expired.
- **Solution**: Go to http://aws.amazon.com and choose **Sign Up Now** to open a new account.

Invalid device name upload. Launching EC2 instance failed.

- **Cause**: The block device mappings in your launch configuration might contain block device names that are not available or currently not supported.
- **Solution**:
  1. Use the describe-volumes command to see how the volumes are exposed to the instance.
  2. Create a new launch configuration using the device name listed in the volume description.
  3. Update your Auto Scaling group with the new launch configuration using the update-auto-scaling-group command.

Value () for parameter virtualName is invalid...

- **Error Message**: Value () for parameter virtualName is invalid. Expected format: 'ephemeralNUMBER'. Launching EC2 instance failed.

- **Cause**: The format specified for the virtual name associated with the block device is incorrect.

- **Solution**:

  1. Create a new launch configuration by specifying the device name in the `virtualName` parameter. For information about the device name format, see Instance Store Device Names in the *Amazon EC2 User Guide for Linux Instances*.

  2. Update your Auto Scaling group with the new launch configuration using the update-auto-scaling-group command.

EBS block device mappings not supported for instance-store AMIs.

- **Cause**: The block device mappings specified in the launch configuration are not supported on your instance.

- **Solution**:

  1. Create a new launch configuration with block device mappings supported by your instance type. For more information, see Block Device Mapping in the *Amazon EC2 User Guide for Linux Instances*.

  2. Update your Auto Scaling group with the new launch configuration using the update-auto-scaling-group command.

Placement groups may not be used with instances of type 'm1.large'. Launching EC2 instance failed.

- **Cause**: Your cluster placement group contains an invalid instance type.

- **Solution**:

  1. For information about valid instance types supported by the placement groups, see Placement Groups in the *Amazon EC2 User Guide for Linux Instances*.

  2. Follow the instructions detailed in the Placement Groups to create a new placement group.

  3. Alternatively, create a new launch configuration with the supported instance type.

  4. Update your Auto Scaling group with new placement group or launch configuration using the update-auto-scaling-group command.

Troubleshooting Amazon EC2 Auto Scaling: AMI Issues

This page provides information about the issues associated with your AMIs, potential causes, and the steps you can take to resolve the issues.

To retrieve an error message, see Retrieving an Error Message.

When your EC2 instances fail to launch due to issues with your AMI, you might get one or more of the following error messages.

Topics

- The AMI ID does not exist. Launching EC2 instance failed.
- AMI is pending, and cannot be run. Launching EC2 instance failed.
- Value () for parameter virtualName is invalid.
- The requested instance type's architecture (i386) does not match the architecture in the manifest for ami-6622f00f (x86_64). Launching ec2 instance failed.

The AMI ID does not exist. Launching EC2 instance failed.

- **Cause:** The AMI might have been deleted after creating the launch configuration.
- **Solution:**
    1. Create a new launch configuration using a valid AMI.
    2. Update your Auto Scaling group with the new launch configuration using the update-auto-scaling-group command.

AMI is pending, and cannot be run. Launching EC2 instance failed.

- **Cause:** You might have just created your AMI (by taking a snapshot of a running instance or any other way), and it might not be available yet.
- **Solution:** You must wait for your AMI to be available and then create your launch configuration.

Value () for parameter virtualName is invalid.

- **Cause:** Incorrect value. The `virtualName` parameter refers to the virtual name associated with the device.
- **Solution:**
    1. Create a new launch configuration by specifying the name of the virtual device of your instance for the `virtualName` parameter.
    2. Update your Auto Scaling group with the new launch configuration using the update-auto-scaling-group command.

The requested instance type's architecture (i386) does not match the architecture in the manifest for ami-6622f00f (x86_64). Launching ec2 instance failed.

- **Cause:** The architecture of the `InstanceType` mentioned in your launch configuration does not match the image architecture.
- **Solution:**

163

1. Create a new launch configuration using the AMI architecture that matches the architecture of the requested instance type.

2. Update your Auto Scaling group with the new launch configuration using the update-auto-scaling-group command.

Troubleshooting Amazon EC2 Auto Scaling: Load Balancer Issues

This page provides information about issues caused by the load balancer associated with your Auto Scaling group, potential causes, and the steps you can take to resolve the issues.

To retrieve an error message, see Retrieving an Error Message.

When your EC2 instances fail to launch due to issues with the load balancer associated with your Auto Scaling group, you might get one or more of the following error messages.

Topics

- Cannot find Load Balancer . Validating load balancer configuration failed.
- There is no ACTIVE Load Balancer named . Updating load balancer configuration failed.
- EC2 instance is not in VPC. Updating load balancer configuration failed.
- EC2 instance is in VPC. Updating load balancer configuration failed.
- The security token included in the request is invalid. Validating load balancer configuration failed.

Cannot find Load Balancer . Validating load balancer configuration failed.

- **Cause 1**: The load balancer has been deleted.
- **Solution 1**:
    1. Check to see if your load balancer still exists. You can use the describe-load-balancers command.
    2. If you see your load balancer listed in the response, see **Cause 2**.
    3. If you do not see your load balancer listed in the response, you can either create a new load balancer and then create a new Auto Scaling group or you can create a new Auto Scaling group without the load balancer.
- **Cause 2**: The load balancer name was not specified in the right order when creating the Auto Scaling group.
- **Solution 2**: Create a new Auto Scaling group and specify the load balancer name at the end.

There is no ACTIVE Load Balancer named . Updating load balancer configuration failed.

- **Cause**: The specified load balancer might have been deleted.
- **Solution**: You can either create a new load balancer and then create a new Auto Scaling group or create a new Auto Scaling group without the load balancer.

EC2 instance is not in VPC. Updating load balancer configuration failed.

- **Cause**: The specified instance does not exist in the VPC.
- **Solution**: You can either delete your load balancer associated with the instance or create a new Auto Scaling group.

EC2 instance is in VPC. Updating load balancer configuration failed.

- **Cause**: The load balancer is in EC2-Classic but the Auto Scaling group is in a VPC.
- **Solution**: Ensure that the load balancer and the Auto Scaling group are in the same network (EC2-Classic or a VPC).

The security token included in the request is invalid. Validating load balancer configuration failed.

- **Cause**: Your AWS account might have expired.
- **Solution**: Check whether your AWS account is valid. Go to http://aws.amazon.com and choose **Sign Up Now** to open a new account.

Troubleshooting Auto Scaling: Capacity Limits

This page provides information about issues with the capacity limits of your Auto Scaling group, potential causes, and the steps you can take to resolve the issues.

To retrieve an error message, see Retrieving an Error Message.

If your EC2 instances fail to launch due to issues with the capacity limits of your Auto Scaling group, you might get one or more of the following error messages.

Topics

- We currently do not have sufficient capacity in the Availability Zone you requested ()....
- instance(s) are already running. Launching EC2 instance failed.

We currently do not have sufficient capacity in the Availability Zone you requested ()....

- **Error Message**: We currently do not have sufficient capacity in the Availability Zone you requested (). Our system will be working on provisioning additional capacity. You can currently get capacity by not specifying an Availability Zone in your request or choosing . Launching EC2 instance failed.
- **Cause**: At this time, Auto Scaling cannot support your instance type in your requested Availability Zone.
- **Solution**:
  1. Create a new launch configuration by following the recommendations in the error message.
  2. Update your Auto Scaling group with the new launch configuration using the update-auto-scaling-group command.

instance(s) are already running. Launching EC2 instance failed.

- **Cause**: The Auto Scaling group has reached the limit set by the `DesiredCapacity` parameter.
- **Solution**:
  - Update your Auto Scaling group by providing a new value for the `--desired-capacity` parameter using the update-auto-scaling-group command.
  - If you've reached your limit for number of EC2 instances, you can request an increase. For more information, see AWS Service Limits.

Auto Scaling Resources

The following related resources can help you as you work with this service.

- **Auto Scaling** – The primary web page for information about Auto Scaling.
- **Auto Scaling Technical FAQ** – The answers to questions customers ask about Auto Scaling.
- **Amazon EC2 Discussion Forum** – Get help from the community.
- ** Classes & Workshops** – Links to role-based and specialty courses as well as self-paced labs to help sharpen your AWS skills and gain practical experience.
- ** AWS Developer Tools** – Links to developer tools, SDKs, IDE toolkits, and command line tools for developing and managing AWS applications.
- ** AWS Whitepapers** – Links to a comprehensive list of technical AWS whitepapers, covering topics such as architecture, security, and economics and authored by AWS Solutions Architects or other technical experts.
- ** AWS Support Center** – The hub for creating and managing your AWS Support cases. Also includes links to other helpful resources, such as forums, technical FAQs, service health status, and AWS Trusted Advisor.
- ** AWS Support** – The primary web page for information about AWS Support, a one-on-one, fast-response support channel to help you build and run applications in the cloud.
- ** Contact Us** – A central contact point for inquiries concerning AWS billing, account, events, abuse, and other issues.
- ** AWS Site Terms** – Detailed information about our copyright and trademark; your account, license, and site access; and other topics.

Document History

The following table describes important additions to the Amazon EC2 Auto Scaling documentation.

Feature	Description	Release Date
Support for target tracking scaling policies	Set up dynamic scaling for your application in just a few steps. For more information, see Target Tracking Scaling Policies for Amazon EC2 Auto Scaling.	12 July 2017
Support for resource-level permissions	Create IAM policies to control access at the resource level. For more information, see Controlling Access to Your Amazon EC2 Auto Scaling Resources.	15 May 2017
Monitoring improvements	Auto Scaling group metrics no longer require that you enable detailed monitoring. You can now enable group metrics collection and view metrics graphs from the **Monitoring** tab in the console. For more information, see Monitoring Your Auto Scaling Groups and Instances Using Amazon CloudWatch.	18 August 2016
Support for Application Load Balancers	Attach one or more target groups to a new or existing Auto Scaling group. For more information, see Attaching a Load Balancer to Your Auto Scaling Group.	11 August 2016
Events for lifecycle hooks	Auto Scaling sends events to CloudWatch Events when it executes lifecycle hooks. For more information, see Getting CloudWatch Events When Your Auto Scaling Group Scales.	24 February 2016
Instance protection	Prevent Auto Scaling from selecting specific instances for termination when scaling in. For more information, see Instance Protection.	07 December 2015
Step scaling policies	Create a scaling policy that enables you to scale based on the size of the alarm breach. For more information, see Scaling Policy Types.	06 July 2015

Feature	Description	Release Date
Update load balancer	Attach a load balancer to or detach a load balancer from an existing Auto Scaling group. For more information, see Attaching a Load Balancer to Your Auto Scaling Group.	11 June 2015
Support for ClassicLink	Link EC2-Classic instances in your Auto Scaling group to a VPC, enabling communication between these linked EC2-Classic instances and instances in the VPC using private IP addresses. For more information, see Linking EC2-Classic Instances to a VPC.	19 January 2015
Lifecycle hooks	Hold your newly launched or terminating instances in a pending state while you perform actions on them. For more information, see Amazon EC2 Auto Scaling Lifecycle Hooks.	30 July 2014
Detach instances	Detach instances from an Auto Scaling group. For more information, see Detach EC2 Instances from Your Auto Scaling Group.	30 July 2014
Put instances into a Standby state	Put instances that are in an `InService` state into a `Standby` state. For more information, see Temporarily Removing Instances from Your Auto Scaling Group.	30 July 2014
Manage tags	Manage your Auto Scaling groups using the AWS Management Console. For more information, see Tagging Auto Scaling Groups and Instances.	01 May 2014
Support for Dedicated Instances	Launch Dedicated Instances by specifying a placement tenancy attribute when you create a launch configuration. For more information, see Instance Placement Tenancy.	23 April 2014

Feature	Description	Release Date
Create a group or launch configuration from an EC2 instance	Create an Auto Scaling group or a launch configuration using an EC2 instance. For information about creating a launch configuration using an EC2 instance, see Creating a Launch Configuration Using an EC2 Instance For information about creating an Auto Scaling group using an EC2 instance, see Creating an Auto Scaling Group Using an EC2 Instance.	02 January 2014
Attach instances	Enable Auto Scaling for an EC2 instance by attaching the instance to an existing Auto Scaling group. For more information, see Attach EC2 Instances to Your Auto Scaling Group.	02 January 2014
View account limits	View the limits on Auto Scaling resources for your account. For more information, see Auto Scaling Limits.	02 January 2014
Console support for Auto Scaling	Access Auto Scaling using the AWS Management Console. For more information, see Getting Started with Amazon EC2 Auto Scaling.	10 December 2013
Assign a public IP address	Assign a public IP address to an instance launched into a VPC. For more information, see Launching Auto Scaling Instances in a VPC.	19 September 2013
Instance termination policy	Specify an instance termination policy for Auto Scaling to use when terminating EC2 instances. For more information , see Controlling Which Auto Scaling Instances Terminate During Scale In.	17 September 2012
Support for IAM roles	Launch EC2 instances with an IAM instance profile. You can use this feature to assign IAM roles to your instances, allowing your applications to access other AWS services securely. For more information , see Launch Auto Scaling Instances with an IAM Role.	11 June 2012

Feature	Description	Release Date
Support for Spot Instances	Request Spot Instances in Auto Scaling groups by specifying a Spot Instance bid price in your launch configuration. For more information, see Launching Spot Instances in Your Auto Scaling Group.	7 June 2012
Tag groups and instances	Tag Auto Scaling groups and specify that the tag also applies to EC2 instances launched after the tag was created. For more information, see Tagging Auto Scaling Groups and Instances.	26 January 2012
Support for Amazon SNS	Use Amazon SNS to receive notifications whenever Auto Scaling launches or terminates EC2 instances. For more information, see Getting SNS Notifications When Your Auto Scaling Group Scales. Auto Scaling also added the following new features: [See the AWS documentation website for more details]	20 July 2011
Scheduled scaling actions	Added support for scheduled scaling actions. For more information, see Scheduled Scaling for Amazon EC2 Auto Scaling.	2 December 2010
Support for Amazon VPC	Added support for Amazon VPC. For more information, see Launching Auto Scaling Instances in a VPC.	2 December 2010
Support for HPC clusters	Added support for high performance computing (HPC) clusters.	2 December 2010
Support for health checks	Added support for using Elastic Load Balancing health checks with Auto Scaling-managed EC2 instances. For more information, see Using ELB Health Checks with Auto Scaling.	2 December 2010
Support for CloudWatch alarms	Removed the older trigger mechanism and redesigned Auto Scaling to use the CloudWatch alarm feature. For more information, see Dynamic Scaling for Amazon EC2 Auto Scaling.	2 December 2010
Suspend and resume scaling	Added support to suspend and resume scaling processes.	2 December 2010

Feature	Description	Release Date
Support for IAM	Added support for IAM. For more information, see Controlling Access to Your Amazon EC2 Auto Scaling Resources.	2 December 2010

www.ingramcontent.com/pod-product-compliance
Lightning Source LLC
LaVergne TN
LVHW082039050326
832904LV00005B/234